Spoken
Language
Difficulties

Spoken Language Difficulties

Practical strategies and activities for teachers and other professionals

Lynn Stuart, Felicity Wright, Sue Grigor and Alison Howey

David Fulton Publishers
London

David Fulton Publishers Ltd
414 Chiswick High Road, London W4 5TF

www.fultonpublishers.co.uk

First published in Great Britain in 2002 by David Fulton Publishers Ltd
Reprinted twice 2003
10 9 8 7 6 5 4 3

British Library Cataloguing in Publication Data
A catalogue record for this book is available from the British Library.

ISBN 1-85346-855-X

Typeset by Textype Typesetters, Cambridge
Printed and bound in Great Britain by The Thanet Press, Margate

Contents

Section 2 Non-verbal difficulties

Section 3 Expressive language difficulties

Notes on contributors

Sue Grigor is Head of the Communication Support Service, Northumberland County Council. She is a teacher, has an MEd in Child Language and Language Disability and is currently completing a PhD in Speech Sciences.

Alison Howey is a teacher with an MEd in Child Language and Language Disability. She is also a qualified teacher of children with hearing impairments.

Lynn Stuart is the principal author of this book. She is also the author of many educational books, including *Reading Writing* (Hodder & Stoughton) and *Cloze Plus* (Hodder & Stoughton), under the name of Lynn Hutchinson, and has contributed to various journals and publications. She is a teacher with a DAES in Child Language and Language Disability.

Felicity Wright is the Senior Teacher of the Communication Support Service, Northumberland County Council. She gained a BSc in Speech Sciences before qualifying as a teacher, and has experience as both a teacher and a speech and language therapist.

Foreword

The success of education in meeting its goals depends on clear and appropriate communication between teacher and pupil. Within the eudcation system, in and out of the classroom, there are many children who struggle to understand and use spoken language. Sometimes these difficulties are clear and obvious, as in the case of a child with severe difficulties in articulating speech sounds. However, frequently the nature of a child's difficulties is unclear. Perhaps the child just does not seem to understand. Perhaps he (usually he) seems to struggle to find words. Perhaps he seems quite articulate but does not relate well to others. Perhaps he just seems to be a wilful or inattentive individual. There are many teachers who struggle to understand the difficulties that their pupils have and the ways in which they can be helped to develop their communication skills to learn and to cope with social interaction with their peers. Unfortunately, there is a serious dearth of professionals, such as teacher therapists, who have expertise in providing advice on these pupils' needs. The opportunity to consult an expert is often delayed for several weeks or months, and, in the meantime, day by day the child is failing to progress, failing to communicate and is building up a history of feelings of inadequacy. The teacher, too, feels unable to cope and knows that she is not meeting the child's needs. Here is a set of resources to help fill that gap. It is designed to help teachers and their assistants in their task of considering, observing and assessing the individual child's communicative strengths, weaknesses and needs for intervention and support. It should prove invaluable in facilitating teachers in their complex task of attempting to achieve successful educational and social inclusion for all pupils.

Marion Farmer, MSc, PhD
Senior Lecturer in Psychology
Chartered Educational Psychologist
Department of Psychology
University of Northumbria
Newcastle-upon-Tyne
November 2001

Preface

Increasing numbers of children are referred to the Northumberland County Council's Communication Support Service for assessment of their language and communication needs, and advice on how to manage their difficulties within class. The authors, who are all specialist peripatetic teachers, respond to these requests. They also work with pupils whose Statements of Special Educational Needs (SEN) identify a communication difficulty, and who have dedicated additional support from an SEN Support Assistant.

This book arose out of the need to create a bank of advice and support materials to help teachers and assistants address specific spoken language difficulties. It is designed to help Special Educational Needs Coordinators (SENCOs) set appropriate targets for Individual Education Plans (IEPs), and provide resources to help the child achieve the targets set when no other additional specialist resource is available in school.

For the sake of clarity alone, in this book we have used 'he' to refer to the child and 'she' to refer to the adult.

Acknowledgements

The authors would like to acknowledge the dedication and commitment of Lesley Atkinson, former Head of Service, to the pupils in her care and thank her for the personal and professional support given to them over many years.

They would also like to acknowledge the outstanding clerical support given to the team, especially that of Pamela O'Brien, whose personal contribution made this book a reality.

In creating this book the authors have drawn on the knowledge and experience of many teachers and therapists shared through courses, workshops and good practice. Much of the book is original. Other parts rest on the development of approaches and strategies in circulation and in the public domain. It has not been possible to trace the source of all the ideas and resources that we have found so valuable and wanted to include in this book. As a consequence there may be material whose originator has not been properly acknowledged and for this we apologise and would seek to correct the omission in a later edition or reprint.

We would like to thank Maggie Johnson, Speech and Language Therapist, for her generosity in allowing us to reproduce materials originally developed by her. These are: pages 95–6, from *Breaking Down the Barriers*, and pages 59–61 and 108–9, from *Functional Language in the Classroom and at Home*.

Thanks are also due to Ann Locke for permission to draw from *Living Language* (see pages 7 and 80).

Introduction

This book is designed to make it easy to identify a child's difficulty and find the relevant page(s) of practical activities which can then be photocopied for use. Simply decide whether the difficulty is primarily to do with the understanding of spoken language; an expressive language difficulty; or a related area which affects language.

The contents page shows the most common difficulties found within these main areas and the page to go to for advice.

Suggested IEP targets are included at the end of each section.

The areas of difficulty have been coded to help organisation and page numbers supplied for ease of reference.

Explanation of the codes used in this book

Section 1 Receptive language difficulties

The first section concerns **receptive language**, which refers to the understanding of language. This section starts with some general information and a checklist to help identify specific areas of difficulty. All the pages begin with the code **R**. Text concerned with the understanding of vocabulary, **receptive vocabulary**, is coded **RV**. **Receptive grammar (RG)** is the understanding of sentence grammar, and **receptive comprehension (RC)** refers to the comprehension of what is heard.

Section 2 Non-verbal difficulties

The second section relates to **non-verbal difficulties** in other areas that affect understanding of language but are not language difficulties. These are **attention and listening (AL)**, and **auditory memory (AM)**.

Section 3 Expressive language difficulties

The third section is concerned with **expression through language**. This includes **expressive language (E)**, **expressive vocabulary (EV)**, and **expressive grammar (EG)**. Difficulties relating to **speech** are included in this section and have the code **S**. Other aspects of communication through language are **play skills** coded **P**, the **uses of language (UL)** and **conversation skills (CS)**.

1 Receptive language difficulties

R1 Understanding in class

The understanding of language checklist (R2) should help to identify the pattern of strengths and weaknesses shown by a particular child. When you have a profile of the child's understanding you can target particular areas as a focus for development. The table below provides a summary of where to look for materials to help the child following completion of the checklist on p.2.

Question no.	Response	Likely area of difficulty	Section
a–k	Yes	Understanding of vocabulary Understanding of grammar Comprehension Auditory memory Attention and concentration	RV RG and EG RC AM AL
l–p	No	Comprehension and thinking skills	RC

You may find that the child experiences difficulties understanding language in all settings. However, some settings can be more helpful than others for some children, particularly as they get older. Looking at how well a child copes, where and with whom, can allow you to pinpoint what is helpful to a child in one setting and attempt to provide these same elements in another.

Factors that contribute to the child doing better in some situations than others include:

- layout of classroom
- adjacent pupils
- opportunities for distraction, such as computers, windows and walkways
- length and appropriateness of teacher talk
- lesson structure
- classroom expectations regarding behaviour, group work, volume of work expected in class, how it is recorded, etc.

R2

Understanding of language checklist

Name of child: .... D.o.B. ....

School: .... Teacher: .... Year group: ....

Date: .... Compiled by: ....

Does the child:	Spontaneously			With support		
	1:1	Small group	In class	1:1	Small group	In class
a) have difficulty following classroom instructions?						
b) need longer to respond than others?						
c) need instructions broken down?						
d) depend on separate instructions?						
e) pick up new vocabulary slowly?						
f) have to be deliberately taught vocabulary?						
g) quickly forget new words?						
h) watch/imitate others in order to carry out instructions?						
i) fail to understand question words, especially 'When', 'Why', 'How'?						
j) have difficulty relating new information to something learned earlier?						
k) respond to part of message only?						
l) make inferences?						
m) understand non-literal language?						
n) make predictions?						
o) appreciate verbal humour?						
p) show awareness of self as member of a group?						

R3 Following classroom instructions

Children have difficulty following classroom instructions for a variety of reasons. They may have attention difficulties which make it hard for them to resist distractions, centre their own thoughts and ideas and stay on task.

Some children appear to be in a world of their own and do not see the purpose of the instruction or realise that it applies to them. If the language used tends to require inference, understanding of non-literal language, the relating of new information to something learned earlier or understanding of verbal humour, then they are likely to misunderstand. They may also miss the main point and become distracted by peripheral details. Other children have a different pattern of behaviour suggesting difficulties in a specific area.

Follow the flow chart to see if there is a pattern to the child's difficulties, the probable reason and the section that is aimed at helping the child overcome these problems.

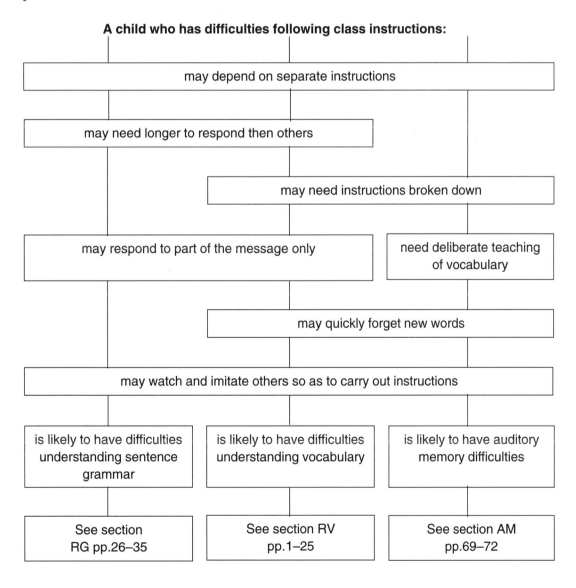

RECEPTIVE VOCABULARY

RV1 Vocabulary development

A child usually develops the concept for something before he names it. For instance, until a child can sort objects according to colour, disregarding shape or function, he will not be able to learn colour names.

To build up a concept, a child will need many experiences in lots of different settings before he can start to recognise the essential qualities that must be present and which make up a particular concept. The experiences must be relevant. The amount of experience each child needs can vary tremendously.

Concept development is helped by the use of language. A child needs to be told words as he experiences what they mean, whether it is naming people and objects; doing actions; recognising abstract properties such as yellow, two, cross, smooth, circle, noisy; or relationships such as big, heavy, below, thin, equal.

A child is more likely to learn a word if there is a need for him to use it and it is relevant to him. This need can be very motivating and gives some point to him learning it and then using it.

When teaching vocabulary, keep your language very simple. The target words should be clear and obvious. The child must be able to understand any other words you use and also the sentence grammar (which should be only marginally more complex than the language he uses).

Teaching tips

- Keep language simple.
- Reduce other distractions.
- Use interesting material/equipment.
- Choose relevant and developmentally appropriate vocabulary items.
- Present the word in many different contexts.
- Do not persist too long – present little and often.
- Continue to reinforce words apparently understood.
- Reward appropriate responses.

RV2 Teaching vocabulary

General vocabulary

These are the three steps necessary to learn and use new words:

1. teacher uses the word
2. child understands the word
3. child uses the word.

General guidelines to bear in mind when teaching early vocabulary:

- teach in groups of children with a similar language level
- teach new vocabulary alongside familiar vocabulary
- keep the learning as active as possible – 'handle' nouns, 'do' verbs
- give time for the child to become familiar with new materials/objects/activities before starting teaching
- always work from concrete to abstract, i.e. follow the sequence: real object/ imaginative play with real object/play with toys or models of real object/ photograph and pictures/songs and stories
- generalise the context so when the child appears to understand the target word in one context, encourage him to use the word in other contexts, and with other people, including those at home (a home/school diary can be useful for this).

Topic vocabulary

Teach this following the general guidelines above.

- It is useful to pre-teach key vocabulary related to subject or topics.
- Check understanding of new words regularly.
- For younger children, illustrated word mats reinforce vocabulary and awareness of things which go together and how they are related.
- Older children benefit from learning key words from banks of topic vocabulary, compiled by subject coordinators in advance of teaching the topic.
- Children can make their own wordbooks of key words (including numeracy words) with their own definitions and illustrations.

Abstract vocabulary

These are words for things that cannot be physically experienced. These words describe the particular qualities things have such as **red, small, heavy, smooth, thin, loud**. Abstract words also describe the relationship between things as in **beside, bigger, next, often**.

- This teaching is best done frequently.
- Introduce only a couple of new words at a time and teach them alongside ones the children already know.
- Remember – children learn from practical experience. If they can 'do' the word they are more likely to remember it.

- Shape, movement and space vocabulary are mainly words they can do: make themselves little (curl up); run fast; be noisy; tiptoe softly; go under or over a chair; stand beside a table, another child (see also Prepositions (p.14) and Spatial vocabulary (p.18)).
- Colour and texture vocabulary can be taught through sorting and matching.
- Number and quantity words can be taught through counting; moving things from one container to another; following instructions – 'give me two red cubes', 'put all the bricks away', 'give me some pennies', etc.
- Time vocabulary can be taught through children doing actions again, twice (see also Time vocabulary (p.20)).
- Role play is useful for learning the vocabulary of personal qualities such as feelings.
- It is harder to grasp abstract words because they are hard to show and do not refer to particular things (e.g. red, all). These words need to be taught not from a single example but by a small range of simple concrete contexts. For example, teach taking something **off** the table, **off** the wall, **off** the teacher's head etc. so the child can grasp what it is common in all these situations. These same few contexts should be repeated constantly until the child shows some understanding of the relevant idea, at which point other more varied and less concrete contexts can be introduced.
- Abstract vocabulary is difficult to grasp and teaching should be slow and careful. It will confuse children if it is extended too quickly into different contexts, especially areas that are less concrete and more abstract.

RV3   Abstract vocabulary checklist

	LEVEL I	LEVEL II	LEVEL III	LEVEL IV
1. QUALITY	like	same/as too	different new very	almost old
2. COLOUR	blue green red	black white yellow	colour orange pink purple	dark/er light/er plain striped
3. TEXTURE	hard soft	cold dry	furry rough smooth warm	
4. SOUND	noisy quiet/ly	loud/ly soft/ly		high low
5. SHAPE	dot/spot line round	circle flat square	cross triangle	corner rectangle curved shape diamond slant/slope oval straight
6. SIZE	heavy little	empty biggest fat full long small	large bigger light fattest short heaviest tall longest thin smallest	deep fatter lightest narrow heavier shortest shallow longer tallest thick smaller thinnest wide largest
7. MOVEMENT	fast slow/ly	moving quick/ly still		jerky smooth
8. QUANTITY	a bit all a lot some	another as much as any many no more	about half other both most every nearly few only	each less plenty enough much several equal none unequal fewest part whole

9. SPACE	by through
	inside under
	off
	out
	over
	to
		around/round
		           next to
		away in front of
		behind outside
		bottom straight
		forwards top
		near
			back
			backwards low
			beside middle
			between/in between
			           side
			far together
			front towards
				high above row
				across sideways
				against upright
				apart
				below
				facing

10. TIME	again now	after soon today	always before later yesterday	early sometimes late tomorrow never twice once
11. NUMBER	one two	three four five first	number second third last	
12. PERSONAL QUALITIES	good happy naughty sad	bad hungry nice pretty	cross frightened kind thirsty	clever excited pleased unkind

Key
x = doesn't understand
u = understands
√ = using

	Updated		Updated		Updated

Adapted from 'Putting Words Together', part of *Living Language* © Ann Locke 1995, by permission of the Author and the Publishers. Published by NFER-Nelson Ltd, Darville House, 2 Oxford Road East, Windsor, Berkshire SL4 1DF.

RV4 Balance of vocabulary

Young children need a balance of vocabulary, including nouns, verbs, pronouns, adjectives, adverbs and prepositions.

- **Nouns** are the names of people, places and things e.g. Mum, bike, dog.
- **Verbs** are 'doing' words such as jump, think, write. They also describe states.
- **Pronouns** take the place of nouns, e.g. 'he' refers to someone named earlier. Others include I, me, her, mine, they, etc.
- **Adjectives** are words that describe the nouns, e.g. blue, pretty, big.
- **Adverbs** add a quality to verbs (and some other words) modifying them in some way, e.g. here, then, last, quickly, nicely.
- **Prepositions** are words that describe the position of one thing in relation to another e.g. in, under, after, with.

Here are some ideas for teaching these kinds of words. Where possible, encourage the child to say the words (as appropriate) at the same time as he is doing the activity, so that use quickly follows understanding.

Verbs

Act out verbs. Let the child instruct others and take turns.

Nouns

- **Naming**. Many names can be taught by naming and asking the child to repeat the name. Then ask, 'Show me a ____', 'Take the ____.'
- **Completion**. After modelling, the child is encouraged to complete items such as, 'This girl is wearing a ____.'
- **Forced alternatives**. Ask, 'Is this a cat or a dog?'
- **Verbal absurdity**. The child must know this is a joke! Say something like (while pointing to a pig) 'This is a cow.' This should provoke the right word. Look at pictures and say, 'This boy is drinking his dinner' (instead of juice) etc.

RV5 Pronouns

- **I/you**. While the child is performing an action, ask 'What are you doing?' Assist him to respond, 'I'm jumping' etc. Reverse roles so he decides your actions, e.g. 'You're sitting.'
- **You**. Take turns being the teacher. The teacher instructs, 'You – jump!' 'You – fall' etc.
- **You/me mine/yours**. Share out objects. 'One for you, one for me', or 'This is mine, this is yours.'
- **Mine/yours**. Ask questions such as 'Whose ball is big?' Response: 'Mine is.' 'Whose shoe is red?' 'Yours is.' Use other children as models.
- **My/your**. Take lotto/bingo cards, saying, 'I've got my fish', or 'I've got your lion.' Take turns.
- **He/she him/her**. Act out, or use toys, and instruct each other, 'She scratches him', 'He pulls her' etc.
- **I/we**.
  Do and say. Use these models; 'I can hop', 'I am jumping', etc.
  I like. 'I like . . .', 'I don't like . . .' etc., with pictures and objects.
- **He/she**.
  Colour the person. Provide outline drawings of a boy or girl (or man or woman). Give instructions using he/she, e.g. 'He has a blue shirt', 'She has brown hair', for the child to colour the pictures accordingly. Then exchange roles so that the child gives instructions using he/she.
  Let's go walkabout. Take the child on a walk around the school. Let him see activities going on and encourage comments using the correct pronouns.
  Action pictures. Provide a set of pictures of a person or animal performing some sort of action. Take it in turns to describe the picture with the words, 'He is digging', etc. A variation is to put a paperclip on each picture. The child then 'catches' a picture with a magnet on a string and has to describe it using the correct pronoun.
  Action noughts and crosses. Place pictures of people (single male, and female) face down in a matrix of nine squares. The child then turns up a picture and if he describes it with the correct pronoun he can then place a nought or cross card in the square. The game can be turned into a game of noughts and crosses.
- **He/she/they**.
  Action noughts and crosses as above, but use pictures of single males, single females, single and mixed sex groups to elicit the correct pronoun.
  Let's go walkabout. Take the child on a walk around the school. Let him see activities going on and encourage comments using the correct pronouns.

RV6 Adjectives

Quality (colour, shape, size, texture, weight)

Follow this sequence to teach any of these adjectives:

1. Show the child a red ball and name it 'A **red** ball' (give adjective and noun). 'This is **red**'
2. Find and name other red objects around the room.
3. Introduce a second colour and repeat steps 1 and 2.
4. Put both red and yellow balls before you. Say, 'Give me the **red** ball.'
5. If he is right, hold out both balls – he must say the correct words and then take the ball.
6. Add more red and yellow objects according to ability.

Adjective boxes

Collect materials for teaching qualities, e.g.:

- **hard/soft**: pencil, stone, marble, cotton wool
- **long/short**: ribbon, shoelaces, string, sticks
- **tall/short**: containers of various sizes
- **straight/curved**: pencils, ruler, fork, hair clips
- **same/different**: mosaic shapes, stickers, 'swap' cards
- **empty/full**: containers empty and full – rice, cereal, stones
- **heavy/light**: feather, ping pong ball, cotton wool, stones, brick
- **open/shut**: paper/card house with windows and doors to open and shut, lock and key
- **pretty/ugly**: plastic monsters, flowers, jewellery, insects
- **shiny**: mirror, tinfoil, jewellery
- **rough/smooth**: stones, pebbles, sandpaper, scourer, silk
- **sharp**: pins, scissors, knife.

Contrast

Use pictures to contrast qualities such as colour, shape and size.

Fresh fruits

- **sticky** date
- **sweet/juicy** orange
- **furry** peach, kiwi
- **fresh/round/juicy** apple
- **sour** lemon
- **prickly** pineapple, etc.

Comparatives and superlatives

Using a group of children, say things such as, 'You are the **tallest/shortest**', 'You have the **longest/shortest** hair' etc. Then compare two children: 'Peter is **taller** than Gary', 'Lisa's hair is **darker** than Jenny's' etc. Ask the children, 'Who is the **shortest/tallest**?' etc.

More comparatives and superlatives

When the child understands these concepts, extend his understanding to other objects, such as:

- string or sticks: **long, longer, longest/short, shorter, shortest**
- cups or balls: **big, bigger, biggest/small, smaller, smallest**
- block towers: **high, higher, highest/low, lower, lowest**
- fruits: **hard, harder, hardest/soft, softer, softest**
- pin/pencils: **sharp, sharper, sharpest**
- pictures of people:
    pretty, prettier, prettiest/ugly, uglier, ugliest
    fat, fatter, fattest/thin, thinner, thinnest
    tall, taller, tallest/short, shorter, shortest
- containers of water: **deep, deeper, deepest/full, fuller, fullest**

Irregular comparisons

good, better, best	**far, further, furthest**
bad, worse, worst	**old, older, oldest**
much, more, most	**old, elder, eldest**
many, more, most	**little, less, least**

RV7 Adverbs

The most common types of adverb are of **place**, **time** and **manner**. Children usually learn them in this order.

Adverbs of **place** include: near/far, here/there, up/down.
Adverbs of **time** include: now, soon, then, today, tomorrow, after, the next day, next, first, last.
Adverbs of **manner** usually end in -ly, e.g. quickly.

Ideas for teaching adverbs of place

near/far

- Use animals, objects, etc. Say, 'I'm putting the car **near** the lorry', 'Put the cow **near** the horse', 'I'm putting the dog **far** away in the corner.'
- Follow instructions such as, 'Stand **near** the cupboard.'
- Explain that far means a long way away. Tell stories, like 'The king lived in a country **far**, **far** away', and '**Far** away, where the sun never shines . . .' etc. After modelling, encourage the child to say the word 'far' when you pause at the appropriate moment.
- Sing nursery rhymes such as 'Tom he was a Piper's Son' (*The Third Ladybird Book of Nursery Rhymes*) which has the refrain, 'Over the hills and **far** away.' Pause, to allow the child to finish the line.

here/there

- Use any constructional toy. Say things like, 'Put it **here**', 'Put it **there**.' (Make sure there is a distance between here and there.)
- Put toys, bricks, etc. back into containers. Have one close to you, one further away, so you can say and encourage the child to use language with the correct use of here and there.

up/down

- Using vehicles and a sloping surface, command the vehicles: 'Bus – come **down**', 'Car – go **up**.' Take turns.
- The child physically climbs up and down (e.g. climbing frame etc.) verbalising as he does it, or following your instructions.
- Recite nursery rhymes such as 'Hickory Dickory Dock' and 'The Grand Old Duke of York'. The child joins in or uses the correct word when you pause.

Ideas for teaching adverbs of time

Now, today, tomorrow, yesterday

- Make a calendar of a week or month. Leave space to illustrate an event for each day. Encourage discussion such as: '**Yesterday**, you did PE', '**Tomorrow**, you will stay for school dinner', 'I am going to Nana's **tomorrow**.' The visual support should help.

Then, after, first, last

Use dolls and household objects. Demonstrate a sequence of everyday activities using dolls and objects, e.g. '**First** the boy wakes up. **Then** he brushes his teeth. **After** that he'll eat breakfast. His sister wakes up **last**.' As you speak the child makes the dolls do what you are describing. You could ask, 'Who woke **first**?', 'What did he do **then**?'

Ideas for teaching adverbs of manner

Use relevant verbs such as walk, beat, colour (in) and choose adverbs such as quickly, slowly, loudly, quietly, neatly, nicely. Instruct the child to 'Walk **slowly/quickly**', 'Beat the drum **loudly/quietly**', 'Colour in **neatly**' etc. Reverse roles. Encourage response to, 'How did Jason walk?', 'Did Katy ask **nicely**?'

RV8 Prepositions

Order of acquisition

Children tend to learn prepositions in this order: prepositions of place (**in** the box), prepositions of time (**after** dinner) and prepositions of manner (**with** a hat).

Teaching prepositions of place

Children usually learn prepositions in the following order:

1. in, on, off, by, inside, out, over, to, up, down
2. around/round, away, behind, near, next to, in front of, outside, on top of
3. back/backwards, beside, between/in between, under
4. above, below, across, through, underneath/beneath, along.

Activities that involve gross motor play are useful for teaching prepositions. You could set up an obstacle course during PE, in the play park or at home using:

Climbing frames:	up/down, on/off
Slide:	up/down
Chairs:	on/under, over, next to/beside
Large boxes:	in/on, behind/in front, beside, between
Tunnels:	through, in, beside/next to
Ladders:	up/down, along
Hoops:	in, out, over, through

Demonstrate the meaning of the preposition and talk about what you are doing. Emphasise the key word e.g. 'under' – 'I'm **under** the table,' or 'on' – 'I'm **on** the chair.' Encourage the child to carry out actions that use the same preposition that you have just demonstrated e.g. 'Go **under** the chair – that's good you're **under** the chair.' Encourage him to say it as he does it.

When the child has learned two or three prepositions tell him to listen carefully – say '**On** the chair', '**under** the chair' etc. Keep the place consistent so only the preposition has to be understood. Gradually increase the range of prepositions you are working on, teaching one or two at a time before you include them in the general activities. Play games that require the child to give you the instructions as well as having to listen to them.

Play hide and seek with toys. Hide some toys around the room and encourage the child to look '**in** the cup', or '**under** the cushion'. Let him have a turn at telling you where to look. During everyday activities, let the child help you 'put the spoon **in** the drawer', or 'the book **on** the shelf'. Draw pictures of furniture or cut pictures from a catalogue. Ask the child to either draw an object or place a picture of an object, either **in/on/under** the pieces of furniture. You can then take it in turns doing this so he can practise using the prepositions too.

Teaching prepositions of time

The first ones to teach are usually:

- **at** (meaning a fixed point in time, e.g. **at** 3 o'clock)
- **on** (meaning a particular day, e.g. **on** Tuesday)
- **in** (meaning periods of time, e.g. **in** the morning)
- **from** (meaning until, as long as, e.g. **from** now, **from** 4 o'clock)
- **to** (meaning until, as long as, e.g. from now **to** dinner time).

Other time prepositions are: until/till, since, before (these can also be conjunctions, which join sentences together).

Ideas for teaching early time prepositions

- **On**. Make a calendar of days of the week and illustrate each day with something typical, e.g. PE, swimming, assembly, library, etc. Then encourage talk such as, '**On** Mondays we have hymn practice', 'What do we do **on** Fridays?'
- **In**. Use pictures or make simple illustrations of events that occur, such as daytime, night-time, the seasons. Encourage talk to include things such as, '**In** the evening – stars shine', '**In** summer – we go to the beach!'
- **At**. Use a clock with hands you can move, illustrations of daily events such as eating, going to school, illustrations of festivals and holidays etc. Ask things such as, 'When do we have dinner?' to elicit the response, '**At** 12 o'clock', and 'When does Santa Claus come?' with the reply '**At** Christmas.'
- **From/to**. Use wind-up toys. Allow the child to wind up the toy and hold it ready to activate. Say, 'Wait, not yet. Let it go **from** now.' Reverse roles. Use a clock with hands you can move. Show pictures or tell a story of daily events indicating the time on the clock. For example, 'John got up at 8 o'clock' (show the time), 'He got ready for school **from** 8 o'clock **to** half past eight.' Or 'Amanda ate her dinner and went out to play **from** 12 o'clock **to** 1 o'clock.' Assist the child to repeat the story.

Teaching prepositions of manner

These are: with, for, from, by.

- **With**. Use dolls, animals, and say, acting out, 'The pig is walking **with** the cow', 'Daddy is walking **with** Mummy' etc. Give the dolls objects to carry, saying, 'The woman is walking **with** the bucket/bag' etc. Use pictures of a single subject with one thing different, for example:

    boy **with** blue trousers   monkey **with** a banana
    boy **with** red trousers   monkey **with** an orange
    boy **with** clean shoes   monkey **with** a long tail
    boy **with** dirty shoes   monkey **with** a short tail

  Turn all the pictures face down. Take turns to pick one and describe it to the others.

Use comb, pen, scissors. Ask questions like, 'What do we do **with** a pair of scissors?' Encourage the children to take turns to ask.

- **For/from**. Use tokens. Share them out saying, 'This is **for** me. This is **for** you.' Vary this by taking them back, saying, 'I'm taking this **from** you.'
- **By**. Use model vehicles, pictures of shops, school, home etc. Say, 'Go to the shop. Will you go **by** car, **by** train, **by** plane?' The child should respond saying, e.g. '**by** car'.

RV9 'Wh' question words

Question words are usually understood in the following order:
what (with nouns), what (with verbs), who, what for, where, when, how, how much, why, whose, which.

When playing games with the child, ask the question first so that the child has the correct model to encourage use as well as understanding.

The following are some ideas to help understanding and use.

Who/what?

- **Who is in . . . ?** Take dolls and a container. The child puts the doll in the container (you pretend not to see). You encourage the child (saying it for him if necessary) to ask, 'Who is in . . . ?' Reverse roles.
- **What's in . . . ?** As above, with objects and a different container. When he can do this, mix the dolls and objects, using who/what appropriately, but keep the dolls and objects in their original containers so they are associated with either who or what.
- **Who's this?** Share out pictures or photographs of people. One child takes a picture and says to the others, 'Guess who is on the card?' Other children respond with, 'Who's that?', 'Is it the clown?' etc. Take turns.
- **What's that?** As above, but use pictures of objects.
- Look at pictures in books, asking questions like, 'What is flying?', 'Who is swimming?'

Where?

- **Hide the object.** The child hides the object. You ask, 'Where's the . . . ?' Reverse roles.
- **On the farm.** Using a model farm, take turns asking, 'Where does the horse go?' etc.
- **Let's find out.** Ask about people/things in school, and go to look for them if the child asks correctly. For example, 'Where are the coats?', 'Where is Mrs X?', 'Where is the book?'

When?

- **Time for dinner.** Use a model farmyard. Line up animals to be fed, but keep several aside. Let the child pretend to feed the animals on the farm, but ask him when the excluded animals can be fed, e.g. 'When can the pig eat?' Answer for him at first, with something like 'now/later/after the duck/before the cow' etc. Then let him choose the animals to be excluded so he can ask you when they are to be fed.

How many/how much?

- **Guess how many.** The child hides counters behind his back (only up to as many as he can count). Ask, 'How many?' He should respond with correct number. Reverse roles.

- **Guess how much**. As above, but use coins. This can be incorporated into a shopping game.
- **How much/many**. Use sound, water, counters etc. Ask questions, taking turns. This can be extended to, 'How far?', 'How fast?'

How?

- **Show me**. Ask, 'How do you jump/dance/hop?' The child demonstrates.
- **How game**. Use materials or pictures. Ask questions such as, 'How can the boy reach the biscuit tin?', 'How can we mend this toy?'
- **Silly how games**. Use pictures and/or objects. The child must know this is a joke. Say things like, 'How can I cut this paper?' Put a picture or object beside the paper, saying, 'With a shoe' (if you have chosen a shoe). Take turns asking and responding giving absurd answers.
- **Verbal absurdities**. Use pictures of verbal absurdities and ask about one of them. The child has to find which one and answer, depending on the picture. For example: 'How does the dog go to the park?' – 'On roller skates.' Change roles.

Why . . . because?

- Use pictures and ask questions such as, 'Why do we eat soup with a spoon?' or 'Why don't we eat soup with a fork?' if the child understands 'don't'.
- Use books, asking questions such as, 'Why did Miss Muffet run away?'

Whose?

- **Whose hat is this?** Use pictures that have objects belonging to particular characters, such as a policeman's hat or a farmer's tractor. Look at one picture at a time and ask, 'Whose hat is this?' Work in a group or take turns.

Which?

- **Choose which one**. Use two balls, bricks etc. and ask, 'Which do you want?' Take turns asking and responding.
- **Collect pairs of objects**. Ask, 'Which ball is biggest?' etc. Take turns.

News time

A group of four or five children will be told they have to ask, using a particular question word, one of the other children about their weekend news. Each asks a question using their word (**what, which, where, when, who**) to elicit information. They all take turns to ask and respond. Vary the question words appropriately.

RV10 Spatial vocabulary

This is also called positional vocabulary. It is a term for words that describe the position of things in space and how they relate to each other as in **under**, **high**, **apart**, **row**.

Assess what the child understands by using the list below or the Abstract vocabulary checklist (p.7). Use this over a period of time – try to set up activities that will show whether the child understands. When you have that information, target the words you want him to learn from the same or the next level. The levels are:

I.   In, on, off, by, inside, out, over, to, up, down.
II.   Around/round, away, behind, near, next to, in front of, outside, on top of.
III. Back/backwards, beside, between/in between, under.
IV.   Above, below, across, through, underneath/beneath.

- At first, this vocabulary is best taught using materials in as physical a way as possible. Some of the words can be taught as contrasts, such as on/off, up/down, above/below.
- The child can jump, climb and physically move himself around, following your instructions. You keep saying the target word(s) as he does the actions. Encourage role reversal so that he instructs you to, 'Put the dolly **on** the table', for example. Make sure he understands the other words in the sentence and that he can cope with the number of information-carrying words (ICWs).
- Encourage the child to move toy animals etc. to your command, 'Put the cow **beside** the pig'. Encourage him to give commands to you and others.
- Use groups of children to teach words such as beside, around, behind, near, next to, in front of, back, backwards. For example, 'Tom, stand **next to** James', 'Philip, walk **backwards**', 'Who is standing **in front of** Meg?'
- Use as many situations and contexts as possible in order to generalise his understanding and encourage him to use the vocabulary as he understands it.
- When teaching the words that express a relationship, such as 'in front of', the child can be taken to see that Philip stands **in front of** Katy, but that Katy is **in front of** someone else, depending on the point of view. Move the child around so that he sees things from others' viewpoints – a skill necessary for thinking at a later level.

'Where?' questions

Designed to reinforce the concept of where, these questions on p.19 can be used verbally or as a written language activity. They can be used with two or more children.

An adult or child reads the question aloud and the others have to take turns to give a correct answer. This can be turned into a game between groups with correct answers scored. Another possibility is to write the answers to some of the questions, cut them up into strips and mix them up in front of the children for them to select the correct response when the **where** question is asked.

'Where?' questions

1. Where do we keep eggs?

2. Where do we buy bananas?

3. Where do you go swimming?

4. Where do people keep money?

5. Where are aeroplanes kept?

6. Where do we keep clothes?

7. Where do you eat dinner?

8. Where do you look for ants?

9. Where are cars mended?

10. Where is the bus stop?

11. Where do you have assembly?

12. Where are attics found?

13. Where do people say their prayers?

14. Where does the Queen live?

15. Where do fish live?

16. Where do rabbits live?

17. Where do you keep your toothbrush?

18. Where do you find flowers?

19. Where is your bed?

20. Where is ice-cream kept?

21. Where are fire-engines kept?

22. Where do you see trains?

23. Where do you wash your hands?

24. Where do you buy sweets?

25. Where do you get your hair cut?

26. Where do you see trains?

27. Where do you buy apples?

28. Where do you see boats?

29. Where are swings and slides?

30. Where do you live?

RV11 Time vocabulary

- This vocabulary often develops slowly because it is abstract and can be difficult to teach. It also depends to a large extent on the child's developmental level. The levels are:
  - I.   again, now
  - II. after, soon, today
  - III. always, before, later, yesterday
  - IV. early, late, never, once, sometimes, tomorrow, twice.

In addition there are the days of the week, months, seasons to be learned, plus words such as morning, afternoon, evening, night, and telling the time.

- Choose vocabulary the child needs to know next, and which is relevant to him. Explain what it means where possible, e.g. **twice** means **two times, tomorrow** is the **day after this** one. In this example he will need to understand the concepts of **before** and **after** and that needs to be taught first. Build on his sense of chronology that things happen in sequence. Use opportunities in school to reinforce time vocabulary.
- Timetables can be useful, as can individual cue cards, to help the child learn time vocabulary. Consider using a daily timetable for him, with his activities for the day written or illustrated. He can mark off or cover up the part of his timetable he has completed. There would be opportunities then to talk about what he did **before** playtime, what he will do **next**, etc.
- Collect seven boxes or pots and label them with the days of the week. In each box put a picture or label of what he does regularly on those days. The picture can be stuck on a stick like a flag. Make three flags labelled **yesterday**, **today**, **tomorrow** and change them at the beginning of each day.
- A calendar for a month can be made that includes symbols showing whether it is a school day or home day. The child can illustrate something which has happened on that day – PE, finishing a book, the weather, etc. This provides opportunities to learn days of the week and see patterns, for instance, he goes swimming **every** Tuesday, his class has held an assembly **twice, next** week it is his birthday, etc. Talk about the **weekend** and things he will do, or has done. This develops the child's time vocabulary as well as encouraging him to use appropriate verb tenses when talking about the past and future.
- Establish a home/school diary so you can talk to him about what happened at home, or what is going to happen, for instance, going to his Grandma's **next** Saturday, going to tea with his friend **yesterday**. Similarly, his parents can ask him about successes and events at school.

Using the calendar

1. Photocopy as many calendar blanks as you need (p.22).
2. With the child, write the name of the month on the top line.
3. With the child, decide on a symbol for school days (such as a book, a stick man walking or a car to show how he comes to school) and a symbol for home (usually a house).

4. Let the child put the **home** symbol in the Saturday and Sunday boxes.

5. If possible, start on the first day of the month. Write **1st** on this line for the appropriate day in one of the top row of squares. For instance, if the 1st is a Wednesday, write 1st on the line in the square under Wednesday on the top line.

6. Continue with **2nd**, **3rd**, **4th** etc. written on the line in the squares until the day you start the calendar. The child may need to copy your ordinal (i.e. sequential) numbers.

7. As appropriate, explain how the ordinal numbers come to be written as they are. Explain that instead of writing the whole word 'first' we take the number **1** and add the last two letters of the word 'fir**st**'. Encourage him to listen to the sounds and explain that these numbers show numbers in order. (Use model animals and make queues, showing which is first, second, third etc.). Explain that for **2nd** we write the number **2** and add the last two letters of the word 'seco**nd**'. Encourage the child to follow this pattern to write the ordinal numbers as you go through the month.

8. Put the school symbol in the box in each square for the days he has to come to school until the present day, taking note of the holidays and days at home through illness.

9. Thereafter, complete a square every day if possible. In the remainder of the square, let the child draw a picture or write a key word concerning something that has happened on that day, e.g. swimming, PE, a special assembly, a visitor, trip out, finishing a reading book – any small achievement. On Mondays, try to find out what the child did at the weekend, for example, went shopping, went to Grandma's, played on his bike etc.

10. If you have a home/school diary, events the child is due to go to can be written in advance, such as a party, going to the pictures/a pantomime/a wedding.

'When?' questions

Used verbally or as a written language activity, these questions on p.23 can be used with one child or between two children or groups. Answers can be written on strips of paper and the children can choose the correct answer from a few put in front of them.

Encourage the children to give the time, or time of day, where possible. For instance, the preferred answer to question 1 would be 'in the evening', rather than, 'when we're dirty'.

Calendar

NAME						
MONTH						
Monday	**Tuesday**	**Wednesday**	**Thursday**	**Friday**	**Saturday**	**Sunday**

'When?' questions

1. When do you have a bath?

2. When do you wake up?

3. When do we eat cereals?

4. When do you wear a coat?

5. When is your birthday?

6. When do we have new shoes?

7. When do we hang up a stocking?

8. When do we go to the doctors?

9. When do we put batteries in a torch?

10. When do you brush your teeth?

11. When does it snow?

12. When do new leaves grow on the trees?

13. When do leaves fall off the trees?

14. When do we change our clothes?

15. When do we eat pudding?

16. When do we have fireworks?

RV12 Categorising

- The child will need to learn the individual concepts before understanding the category, although they can often be taught at the same time. It can be useful to refer to the category as a family as he may have some understanding of that.
- At an early stage he should physically group things together, e.g. food, vehicles, plants, furniture, animals. These can be real items, models or pictures.
- When he can sort according to function or attribute, he can be taught sub-categories, such as fruit, vegetable, chairs, cars, farm animals.
- Make pictures of categories, e.g. food. Make subsets of pictures of fruit, vegetables, meat, cereals, fish, dairy produce. The child can stick on, or draw the items.
- Make mobiles of pictures in a particular category, e.g. car, lorry, train, motorbike, referring all the time to that category, 'the vehicle mobile', 'the furniture mobile' etc.
- Collect pictures of shops – e.g. sports shop, bread shop, grocer, florist, shoe shop, toy shop – with some pictures or objects that could be bought there. Encourage him to match them to the right shop. Older children can use shopping catalogues and find particular items, e.g. beds in the 'furniture' section, balls in 'sports' or 'toys', kettles in 'kitchens'.

RV13 Receptive vocabulary: IEP targets

These should be Specific, Measurable, Achievable, Relevant, Timed (i.e. **SMART**).
Choose the most appropriate from the list below:

- **understand abstract vocabulary to Level I/II/III/IV** (*see RV2*)
- **understand a balance of vocabulary to include**
  (*for example*)
  - nouns/verbs – *specify number, type or from list/level used – see RV3 (p.7) and RV4 (p.8)*
  - pronouns – *specify which ones – see RV5 (p.9)*
  - adjectives – *specify which ones – seeRV6 (pp.10–11)*
  - adverbs – *specify which ones – see RV7 (pp.12–13)*
  - prepositions – *specify which ones – see RV8 (pp.14–15)*
- **understand abstract vocabulary related to time** – *see RV11* (pp.20–23)
  (*for example*)
  - again, now
  - after, soon, today
  - always, before, later, yesterday
  - early, late, never, once, sometimes, tomorrow, twice
- **understand abstract vocabulary related to space** – *see RV10* (pp.18–19)
  (*for example*)
  - in, on, off, by, inside, out, over, to, up, down
  - around, away, behind, next to, in front of, outside, on top of
  - back/backwards, beside, between/in between, under
  - above, below, across, through, underneath, beneath
- **understand abstract vocabulary related to size** – *see RV6* (pp.10–11)
  (*for example*)
  - heavy, little
  - empty, full, fat, long, small, biggest
  - large, light, short, tall, thin, bigger
  - deep, narrow, shallow, wide, thick
- **understand question words** – *see RV9* (pp.16–17)
  (*for example*)
  - who, what, what for, where
  - when, how, how much
  - why . . . because, whose, which
  - how, when
- **understand categories** (*specify which ones*) – *see RV12* (p.24)

RECEPTIVE GRAMMAR

RG1 Processing spoken language

Some children need longer to process spoken language than most others. This may be because:

- All thinking processes are slow.
- The child is slow providing a context in which to understand the information given. For instance, the statement 'Stephen saw a big cat' will be understood differently depending on whether the context is the park or the zoo. Some children are slower than others in evaluating the context and then rejecting it for an alternative or less obvious one.
- The child is slow processing sounds into words and vice versa.
- The child has poor auditory memory skills and quickly forgets part or all of the instruction.
- The child may only be able to process a limited number of information-carrying words.
- Some sentence constructions require more processing than the child can cope with.
- The child has sound discrimination difficulties.
- The child has listening and attention difficulties.

If information is presented more quickly than the child can process it, there is a breakdown in understanding resulting in:

- cumulative misunderstanding
- missing 'bits' of information
- 'switching off'.

In all cases, reduce the:

- amount of information
- rate the information is presented.

If children have difficulty processing sentence grammar:

- keep sentences short – this keeps them simple
- pause between sentences.

Remember that:

- Children first understand things in the order they happen. They will therefore find it difficult to follow instructions presented in a non-chronological order, such as, 'Before you paint your picture put your apron on.'
- Children find it difficult to understand reversible passive sentences, such as, 'The boy is chased by the dog', understanding it as, 'The boy chased the dog.'
- Other examples of sentence grammar many children find difficulty understanding include relative clauses such as 'the girl likes the dog, who is friendly', and interrupting constructions such as, 'the dog the girl likes is friendly'.

RG2 Plurals

Most children show awareness of plurals from quite an early age. However, some children do not always respond accurately, particularly if they have experienced intermittent hearing loss through 'glue ear', or have phonological difficulties that make it difficult for them to discriminate the 's' sound, particularly in consonant clusters such as 'ts' (as in 'cats). Sometimes these children do not produce the 's' sound in their speech and in some cases seem unaware of it.

Awareness of 's' sound

Listen for 's'. Give the child a container, ask him to listen for 's' sounds at the ends of words and put a counter in the pot when he hears one. Tell him a story with several plural 's' sounds in, such as: Tom got out of bed. He got washed. He put on a clean T-shirt. He put on trousers. Then he put on socks and shoes. He went down the stairs and ate some cornflakes with milk. Then he put two apples in his bag for playtime. The bell rang two times. Philip and Gary had called for him. He went up the road with his friends.

Ideas for teaching plurals

- **Give me**. Collect objects/pictures of single and several objects or animals. Say, 'Give me the picture of . . . (the cat, or the cats for example). Encourage the child to ask. Sometimes give him the wrong one, and encourage him to correct you.
- **I went to market**. Using objects, take turns to 'buy' one or more objects, saying, 'I went to market and bought a sweet/two sweets' etc.
- **Draw one or more**. Divide two pieces of paper into four or six squares. Edge the squares with different colour crayons. With a barrier between two children, ask them to take turns telling each other to draw a specific number of shapes/letters/fruit etc. in a specific square, using words such as, 'Find the red square. Draw two circles', 'Draw three apples in the green square.' (Make sure the children understand the number vocabulary, such as one, two, three, some, lots of.) This should encourage a developing awareness of plurals.

RG3 Negatives

These are usually best taught using a contrast with the positive, e.g. is/isn't, do/don't.

1. (a) **Is/it's not/isn't**. Using objects known to the child, display one at a time saying, 'This **is** a car', encouraging the child to say the target utterance. Follow this by misnaming an article, e.g. saying, 'This is a car', while showing a teddy. Encourage him to correct you with, 'No, **it's not**' (or 'No **it isn't**') and say what it is.

   (b) Get the child to hide an object (pretend not to see) and then ask something like, 'Is it a ball?' The child should then answer, 'Yes it is', or 'No **it's not**'. You model it for him to start with.

   (c) Use pictures. Point to people/animals in the picture, modelling something like, 'The woman is walking. She**'s not** sitting down.' Point to other people saying, 'He**'s not** sleeping', etc. Encourage the child to say something that the person, animal, **isn't** doing.

   (d) As above, but say things like, 'The dog is sleeping' (when it is eating) to encourage the child to say, 'It**'s not** sleeping.' Make sure he knows it is a joke.

2. **Do/don't**. Model and use role reversal to instruct each other performing actions, such as, 'Do run', '**Don't** run/jump/sit', etc.

3. **Has/hasn't**. Use dolls, teddies etc. and give them hats, bags, scarves etc. saying things like, 'The teddy has a hat, but the doll **hasn't** got a hat', and, 'The woman **hasn't** got a bag. You give her one.' Encourage the child to use the negatives by reversing roles.

RG4 Passive sentences

Children understand active sentences first, i.e. sentences that show the order in which things happen. For instance, 'Fred chopped down the tree.' The subject of the sentence (Fred) then does the action (chop down) and what he does it to (the free).

Passive sentences develop late. They are used when it is more interesting to stress the thing that is being done, rather than the person doing the action. They are also used when no-one knows, or it does not matter, who did the action, as in:

The books **were given** out.
The window **was broken** and the room was cold.

Passive tense verbs are formed by using one of the forms of the auxiliary verb '**be**', as in:

(Singular) The apple **has/had been** eaten.
The apple **is being** eaten.
The apple **will be** eaten.
The apple **was eaten**.
The apple **is going to be** eaten.

(Plural) The apples **have/had been** eaten.
The apples **were** eaten.
The apples are **going to be** eaten.

If the person who carries out the action is mentioned after the passive verb, then '**by**' is used, but in front of it, as in:

The bike was ridden **by** John.
The tree was chopped down **by** Fred.

If materials are responsible for the action, then '**with**' is used:

The glass was filled **with** water.
The bucket was filled **with** sand.

Ideas to teach understanding of passive sentences

Passive with 'by'

Use model dolls to act as the subjects of the sentence; model objects such as fruit, animals, etc. to act as objects of the sentence. Show active sentences first, saying, 'Daddy cuts the apple.' Then say, 'The apple cuts Daddy', making it look silly. Model the correct form in the passive voice, 'The apple **is cut by** Daddy.'

Vary the items, start the sentence and assist the child to say the target utterance. 'The banana . . . (**is eaten by** Mummy/the girl/the dog, etc.)', 'The horse . . . (**is ridden by** etc.).

Help the child to complete the sentence on his own. He may need you to cue him by pointing to the object first to remind him it comes before the subject. Vary the tense, using past, present and future.

Creature food

Depending on the age of the child, use objects and models, pictures or word lists. The pictures and lists should show creatures such as: hen, hedgehog, mouse, duck, dog horse, cat. Their food would be: corn, bread, cheese, a snail, a bone, grass, a mouse.

The child has to show which animal eats which food. If using objects, put them together. Pictures and word lists can be joined with a line. Then encourage the child to talk about what has happened, using the model, 'The grass **was eaten by** the horse', 'The cheese **was eaten by** the mouse.'

Finish the sentence

Ask the child to finish these sentences, then draw a picture to go with each one. If appropriate, write/copy the sentence under each picture.

Sentence: The girl **is chased by** the _____.

The car **is pushed by** the _____.

The cow **is pushed by** the _____.

RG5 Relative clauses

Relative clauses start with **who** (for a person), **which** or **that** (for things and places). The clause, which is like a mini-sentence, is added at the end or can be fitted into the middle of a main sentence. The 'who', 'which' or 'that' always refers to the noun just before it.

These are relative clauses put at the end of a main sentence:

The man is in the car **that is red**.
The postman chased the dog **which is big**.
The dog jumps up at the boy **who is scared**.

Ideas for teaching relative clauses

- **Give me**. Get together an assortment of coloured bricks, cars, etc. Say, 'Give me the brick which is red' etc. Reverse roles, encouraging the child to use the words 'which is'. This can be varied with big and little toys, as in, 'Give me the doll **which is big**'.
- **Which one sir?** Use pictures or cards of faces of various people with no hair, curly/straight/long/short hair, big/little/flat/pointed noses, thick/thin eyebrows, smiling/scowling, with glasses, beards, moustaches, earrings, etc. Say one of the people is a robber. You take the role of the policeman and say, 'Which one, sir?' The child is supposed to identify the robber using the pattern, 'The man **who has** long dark hair', 'The man **who has** glasses', etc. You may have to model and use other children, reversing roles.

RG6 Interrupting constructions

Main sentences can be interrupted in some ways. Interruptions can be hard for children to process because the subject is separated from the verb. For instance, the sentence, 'The school is old', can be interrupted in many ways, such as:

The school **down the road** is old.
The school **my child goes to** is old.
The school, **but not the church**, is old.

This main sentence has been interrupted using phrases. In each case the phrase refers to the noun just before it, i.e. the school, in this case. Sentences can also be interrupted by (usually relative) clauses. They, too, describe the noun just before the interrupting relative clause, e.g. The school, **which is old**, is down the road.

Ideas for teaching interrupting constructions

- **Where's the mouse?** Have pictures of, for example, a mouse under, on, beside a table, under/on a chair, in a box. All the mice must look different, e.g. big spotty, little spotty, big/little white, big/little black etc. or use a toy animal and put it in different places. Then say, 'Where's the mouse?', encouraging the response, 'The mouse **in the box** is big and spotty', 'The mouse **under the table** is black', etc. You may have to model the response you want. It may help if you say, 'The mouse is big and white' then repeat the sentence again, allowing time for the child to interrupt with, '**on the chair**' etc. This game can be played with several children.
- **Don't interrupt!** Make sure the children know this is a game! With a group of children tell them a sentence, such as, 'The girl fell off her bike.' Ask them what could have happened to the girl to make her fall off her bike. Take responses. Tell them you want them to be ready to say their bit as soon as you pause after you have said the word 'girl' but they must say 'who' at the beginning of their bit of the sentence. Practise '**who** drove too fast', '**who** had a puncture', '**who** hit a dog', etc. Then say (jokingly), 'Don't interrupt! The girl (pause for the first contribution) fell off her bike.' Pretend to be cross that you have been interrupted. Make sure all the children have a turn. Roles can be reversed. Other sentences suitable for interruption would be:
    The boy/ . . . /was late for school. The book/ . . . /was wet.
    The dog/ . . . /chased the postman. The girl/ . . . /was crying.

Other ideas can be found in Relative clauses (p.31).

RG7 Comparatives

First the child has to understand the attribute or property associated with an item. For instance, he needs to understand 'tall' before he understands 'taller than'.

- Follow this sequence to teach properties:
  a) Show the child a big teddy and name it. 'A **big** teddy. This is **big**.' Give adjective (big) and noun (teddy). Find and name other big objects around the room.
  b) Introduce a second word, such as 'little'. A contrasting word helps to play up the difference. Go through steps a) and b). Put the big and little teddies before you. Say, 'Give me the **big** teddy.'
  c) If he is correct, hold out both teddies before you. He must say the correct words '**big** teddy' then take the teddy.
  d) Add more big and little objects (spoons, cups, plates, bricks, balls etc.).
  e) Ask him to sort according to size, saying, 'Let's put the **big** ones here.'
- When the child understands the property, he needs to learn how to relate two objects according to property:
  a) Take two objects of different size, saying, for example, 'This teddy **is bigger than** this one. Which one **is bigger**?' The child can point. Ask him to repeat (if he can) 'This one **is bigger**.' Repeat with pairs of bricks, cars etc.
  b) Take a small teddy. Ask the child, 'Which teddy **is bigger**? Let him choose from a pile of mixed up toys (including at least one bigger teddy!).
  c) Take two objects of different size. Ask, 'Which **is bigger**?' When he points/says it correctly, say, 'Yes, the red brick **is bigger than** the blue brick.' Do this several times with different objects.
  d) Ask him which is the bigger of two objects, e.g. car, box.
  e) Take him around the room. Say things like, 'That table **is bigger than** . . .' Encourage him to give a suitable answer.
  f) Encourage him to reverse roles, saying, 'That chair **is bigger than** . . .' and you supply the answer.
  g) Look at books and pictures, saying, 'Show what **is bigger than** that cat', 'Which (of two) tree **is bigger**?' etc.
  h) Draw some pictures of objects in his environment, such as a big teddy and a little mouse, a boat and a shoe, a box and a dice. Ask him to point to the picture saying, 'Show me (*pause*) the teddy which **is bigger than** the shoe.' Repeat with other pictures.
  i) Show him two pairs of objects, such as a big box and a little brick, and a big brick and a little box. Place each pair of objects on different trays, pieces of paper etc. Ask him, 'Show me – the brick which **is bigger than** the box.'
  j) From a mixed pile of objects, say, 'Show me – the dog which **is bigger than** the cup' etc. Encourage turn-taking with you or other children.
  k) Give him two, then three, then four pictures and ask him to show which one is bigger or smaller, e.g. 'the train which **is bigger than** the car'. The other pictures could be of a train bigger than a car/a train smaller than a car/a train the same size as a car. Take turns and play with other children.

Use this pattern to teach other comparatives such as hard/soft, long/short, tall/short etc. See adjective boxes for ideas of materials to use in RV6. There are also other ideas for teaching comparatives on the same advice sheet.

RG8 Information-carrying words

Some children are slow to understand words in a sentence. They tend to respond to a noun and if this is heard within a predictable sentence they may appear to understand more than is really the case. Try to devise situations which they can't guess at and which tell you how many words they can really understand across a range of situations. Start with establishing understanding of two information-carrying words first.

Teaching ideas

Ask the child to do the following things, then repeat the pattern using other words within his understanding. You can perform the action first and get him to copy, repeating what you say. Encourage him to say what he is doing first, to ensure use as well as understanding. When he understands, you can get him to ask another child to perform the action.

Two information-carrying words

Combinations	*Examples*
object + place	put the **brick** on the **table**
object + person	give **Sam** the **cup**
	that's the **dog's house**
action + object	**kick** the **ball**
action + person	**kiss teddy**
person + action	**baby sleeps**
action + place	**sleep** on the **bed**
negative + object	**no coat**
attribution + object	**dirty face**
	red balloon
	little car etc.

Three information-carrying words

Combinations	*Examples*
object + preposition + place	put the **shoe under** the **table**
	put the _____ **beside** the ____ etc.
action + object + person	**throw** the **ball** to **Ben**
person + action + place	make **teddy jump** on the **bed**
	the **cat runs** into the **house**
	the **dog sleeps** under the **table** etc.
action + person + place	**wash Sarah's face**
object + attribution + place	put the **spoon** in the **little box**
	put the **fork** in the **red pan** etc.
person + attribution + object	**John** has a **red coat**
action + attribution + object	**wash** the **dirty cup**
action + attribution + place	**stand** by the **green door**

RG9 Receptive grammar: IEP targets

These should be **S**pecific, **M**easurable, **A**chievable, **R**elevant, **T**imed (i.e. **SMART**).
Choose the most appropriate from the list below:

- **understand plurals** – *see RG2* (p.27)
- **understand negatives** – *specify which ones* – *see RG3* (p.28)
  (*for example*)
    - is not/it's not/isn't, don't, hasn't
- **understand passive sentences** – *see RG4* (pp.29–30)
- **understand relative clauses** – *see RG5* (p.31)
- **understand interrupting constructions** –*see RG6* (p.32)
- **understand comparatives** – *specify which ones* – *see RG7* (p.33) *and RV6* (p.11)
  (*for example*)
    - between two items, e.g. bigger than, bigger (also with large, short, tall, light, thin, heavy, long, small, etc.)
    - between three or more items, e.g. big, bigger, biggest (also with large, short, tall, thin, light, heavy, long, small, etc.)
    - irregular comparatives (such as good, better, best – *specify*)
- **understand sentences containing two/three/four 'bits' of information** – *specify how many*) (see RG8, p.34)

COMPREHENSION

RC1 Understanding spoken language

Children who have a reasonable understanding of vocabulary and sentence grammar for their age may still experience difficulties understanding language beyond the single sentence level. These difficulties may relate to:

- **Poor attention and listening skills.** The child may have problems screening out visual and auditory distractions including his own thoughts and feelings, and have difficulty staying on topic. Suggestions to help improve these skills are given in Section 2 (AL).
- **Poor auditory memory skills.** These include a poor memory span, and difficulties remembering sequences. Suggestions to help improve these skills are given in Section 2 (AM).
- **Slow processing ability.** It may be that the child does not have sufficient time to process one 'bit' of information before another is presented, in which case:
  - slow down the rate of information
  - reduce the amount of information given at one time
  - use visual supports where possible, such as pictures, key words, flow charts.
- **Lack of skill** in the operations needed to make connections between sentences. An example of this is connected discourse, in which talk is extended and meaning is cumulative.

Some of the operations a child may need to carry out to understand extended talk:

- Names and places need to be remembered. Sometimes a child will jump to a conclusion about a name that will divert him. For instance, some children hearing a story about an animal called Barney will assume it is a dinosaur, because of a fictional character on TV, disregarding other information.
- Factual information needs to be remembered.
- The sequence of information given may be very important. The child has to decide if it is important and remember the sequence correctly.
- Some information may be less important than other bits, so the child has to prioritise and decide what is relevant. Sometimes children miss the point and get caught up with irrelevant details.
- Some information may only make sense when the next piece is given, so the child has to 'hold' it all in his mind, amending an earlier hypothesis in the light of further information.
- Information needs to be processed in a context so the child must supply the right one and be prepared to modify or change it. For instance, 'Henry has a big cat' will be understood differently if the conversation is between children or big game hunters.
- The child may need to anticipate and make predictions as to what will happen next.
- The child may have to interpret non-literal language such as figures of speech, similes, metaphors, sayings and clichés.
- The child may have to recognise and understand a variety of language uses, such as white lies, sarcasm, irony, puns and persuasion, in which the meaning is not conveyed by the literal meaning. This involves awareness of others' intentions.
- The child may need to go beyond the facts presented in order to make sense of what he hears. This involves the higher order skills of deduction and inference.

RC2 Extended talk

The following are ideas to help a child understand connected discourse, where talk is extended and meaning is cumulative.

- Give a purpose for listening as this will give the child a focus. Tell him what he will be expected to know or do afterwards.
- Pre-teach difficult or specialist vocabulary, plus names and places. This will reduce the likelihood of a memory overload.
- Give 'signposts' throughout the instruction, saying what the next bit is about, why it is important, etc. For example, 'So far you have been told . . .', 'To sum up . . .', 'The next problem is . . .' This helps to break the discourse up into chunks and directs the child's thinking processes.
- Pause between chunks of information and ask what the child thinks will come next to encourage anticipation and prediction. Then encourage modification of the original hypothesis in the light of further information.
- Encourage recall of facts and sequences. Ask questions such as, 'What was the first thing Theseus did?' Continue with questions about what came next, and how the story or instruction ended.
- Use a storyline or mindmap, making sure all the facts are included in the right order.
- Use written or pictorial support where appropriate. This can make it easier for the child to make connections.
- Explain figures of speech, such as idioms, similes, metaphors etc. Be ready to explain the meaning of non-literal language (see pp.40–8).
- To help him grasp the main point, ask the child to give the information a title. This will help the child to prioritise.
- Encourage summarising by giving the child a postcard (or piece of postcard-sized paper) and tell him he has to write down the most important points in the right order.
- Encourage awareness of the different purposes of language (see pp.38–39).
- Encourage awareness and use of inference through questioning and activities (see pp.49–54).

RC3 Others' language purposes

As children mature, they become more aware that people use language for a wide range of purposes. They understand that people do not always tell the truth, for instance, when they make a joke or tell a lie. Because these are things they do themselves, they can recognise it when others use language for the same purpose.

As they get older they need to recognise that people may deliberately not speak the truth for other purposes. Some children may not recognise when this is the case – they may simply ignore any contradiction and take what is said literally. Others become confused, some become angry, seeing these false statements as lies. For instance, a child may get very upset if someone says, 'good morning!' when it is the afternoon.

When these situations arise, be aware that the child may have difficulty understanding the intention behind what is said, such as to deceive, conceal, persuade or shock. The child who has difficulty understanding the intentions of others usually does not use his own language for these purposes.

Ask the child, 'Is what . . . said true? Why did he/she say it?' You will have to explain the purpose of what was said. Using role play and changing roles may help the child extend his awareness of language uses.

The following are scenarios of some language uses that the child may not understand. For instance, if the child cannot say why the white lie was said, encourage him to understand both the parent's and the child's point of view through role play of each character.

Scenarios

Lie (Purpose: to deceive)

Mark's mother was talking on the telephone. He started throwing his trainer for his dog to catch and bring back. Then he threw too hard and too far. He knocked his mother's favourite vase off the windowsill. When his mother came in and asked how her vase had got broken, Mark said, 'The dog did it. It wasn't my fault!'

White lie (Purpose: lie to avoid hurting someone's feelings)

Kevin asked his mother for a Playstation for his birthday. When the big day came, he unwrapped the box and inside was a football strip, which he did not really want. Still, when his mother asked him if he liked his present, he said, 'Yes, thank you. It's just what I wanted.'

Persuasion (Purpose: manipulate someone so they do as you want)

Mrs Brown's cat had kittens. She did not want to keep them, although she loved cats and would never hurt them. When they were big enough to go to new homes, she put a notice in the shop. Jane saw it and went to see Mrs Brown because she wanted a little black kitten. The only kitten left was a tabby, and Jane didn't want it. But Mrs Brown said, 'If I can't find a home for it soon, it will have to be put to sleep.'

Irony (Purpose: say the opposite of what you mean to surprise another into understanding)

Ross came back from playing football covered in mud. When he opened the door, his mother said, 'I don't think you played football today, you look far too nice and clean!'

Sarcasm (Purpose: to sneer, or make you feel worthless)

Brett got all his spellings wrong. The teacher marked the test and said, 'Everyone give Brett a clap. He's the best speller in the class.'

Double bluff (Purpose: to deceive)

Scott knew his sister had got him either a computer game or a CD for his birthday. He knew his sister wanted to keep it a secret so would tell him a lie. She really had got him a CD. He asked her, 'Have you got me a CD?' and she said, 'Yes.' What did he expect to unwrap on his birthday?

RC4 Figures of speech

Figures of speech, such as similes, metaphors, idioms, sayings and proverbs and clichés, are incomprehensible to a child when taken literally. The child needs to be encouraged to ask when he is confused by what is said, so that the real meaning can be explained.

- **Attributes**. Children need to understand attributes before they can understand similes and metaphors (see RC5).
- **Similes**. The simplest figure of speech is probably the simile – the comparison of one thing with another of a different kind, saying it is **like** or **as** something else. Common similes are: '**as** bright **as** day'; '**like** a ship in sail'; '**as** black **as** coal'; '**like** a cat on hot bricks' (see RC6).
- **Metaphors** are like similes but they say or suggest one thing **is** another, rather than like another. Some will be heard in spoken language, such as, 'You're a dead man.' Most will be encouraged in imaginative and poetic writing (see RC7).
- **Idioms** often cause confusion. Children are unlikely to make these up but need to learn to recognise them. Examples include: 'pull your socks up'; 'in hot water'; 'hold your horses'; 'too big for your boots'.
- **Sayings** and **proverbs** can cause difficulties. Again, children need to recognise them and ask if they don't understand. Examples include: 'out of sight, out of mind'; 'absence makes the heart grow fonder'; 'no smoke without fire'.
- **Clichés**, which have little meaning and are often pompous and unnecessarily wordy, can cause difficulties. Examples are: by and large (meaning generally or usually); at this point in time (meaning now); until such time as (meaning when); in the order of (meaning about). These are best explained as they arise.

RC5 (Activity 1) Attributes

1. Pins and scissors are both .... ? (sharp)
   What else is .... ? (sharp)
   A ....

2. Crying babies and fireworks are both .... ?
   What else is .... ?
   A ....

3. You can .... windows and eggs.
   What else can you .... ?
   A ....

4. The sun and a fire are both .... ?
   What else is .... ?
   A ....

5. Ice-cream and snow are both ....
   What else is .... ?
   A ....

6. Silver and diamonds are both ....
   What else is .... ?
   A ....

7. Wet floors and mud are both ....
   What else is .... ?
   A ....

8. Sports cars and trains are both ....
   What else is .... ?
   A ....

9. Cats and foxes are both ....
   What else is .... ?
   A ....

10. Candyfloss and glue are both ....
    What else is .... ?
    A ....

11. A CD and a coin are both ....
    What else is .... ?
    A ....

12. A snail and a slug are both ....
    What else is .... ?
    A ....

| shiny | slippery | fast | hot | sharp | noisy |
| furry | sticky | slow | break | round | cold |

RC5 (Activity 2) Attributes

More ideas for understanding attributes are:

- **Guess what I am**. Tell the child he is an object and has to respond to questions, such as:
    (pair of scissors)
    What are you made of?
    Where would people keep you?
    What are you for?
    (fork)
    Where would we find you?
    What are you for?
    Can we eat soup/biscuits/ice-cream with you?
    (chair)
    How many legs do you have?
    Where would we find you?
    What are you for?
    (bird)
    Where do you live?
    Who would be afraid of you?
    How do you move?

This can be varied if the child chooses what object or person he is. Others have to guess by asking him questions.

- Ask the child to name several objects with one attribute in common. For example:
    - How many round things can you name?
    - How many heavy things can you name?
    - How many sharp things can you name?
    - How many sticky things can you name?
    - How many poisonous things can you name?

RC5 (Activity 3) Attributes

Making connections

Ask the child to say, or write, responses to the following:

1. In what ways are a cat and mouse alike?
   Say what they **both** have and what they **both** do.
   (fur, whiskers, four legs, tails/run, make noises, can be pets)
2. In what ways are a chair and a table alike?
   Say what they **both** have and where you find **both** of them.
   (four legs/in a house – furniture)
3. In what ways are a toothbrush and a scrubbing brush alike?
   Say what they **both** have and what they are **both** for.
   (bristles, handles/for cleaning)
4. In what ways are a horse and a bike alike?
   Say what they **both** have and what they are **both** for.
   (somewhere to sit (seat, saddle)/for riding)
5. In what ways are a bus and an aeroplane alike?
   Say what they **both** have and what they are **both** for.
   (have an engine, seats, people/to take people on journeys)
6. In what ways are a sock and a glove alike?
   Say what they are **both** for, and what they are **both** made from.
   (to protect/can be made of wool/cotton)
7. In what ways are a pen and pencil alike?
   Say what they **both** look like and what they are **both** for.
   (thin with something in the middle/holding in hand, writing)
8. In what ways are a book and a television alike?
   Say what you can do with **both** of them, and what they **both** have.
   (look at them/learn from them, be told stories)
9. In what ways are a fire and the sun alike?
   Say what they **both** have and how they are **both** used.
   (light, heat/can be used for heating water (solar panels))
10. In what ways are a strawberry and chocolate alike?
    Say what they have **in common** and what they are **both** for.
    (sweet/food)
11. In what ways are a flower and a tree alike?
    Say what they **both** have and where you would find them.
    (roots, stem, leaves/grow)
12. In what ways are snow and rain alike?
    Say what they are **both** made of and where they **both** come from.
    (made of water/come from the sky)
13. In what ways are hair and fingernails alike?
    Say what you can do with **both** of them and where you can find **both** of them.
    (can be cut/on a person)
14. In what way is a knife and a pair of scissors alike?
    Say what they are **both** made of and what you can do with **both** of them.
    (made of metal/can cut)
15. In what way is a window and an egg alike?
    Say what you can do with **both** of them.
    (can break)

16. In what way is a sack and a bag alike?
    Say what you do with **both** of them.
    (carry things)
17. In what way is a tree and a mountain alike?
    Say what you can do to **both** of them.
    (climb them)
18. In what way is a candle and a torch alike?
    Say what they are **both** for.
    (give light)
20. In what way is an orange and pear alike?
    Say what you can do with **both** of them.
    (eat them)

RC6 (Activity 1) Similes

We can describe things by comparing them with something else. We say they are **like** or **as** something else. For instance, if someone is very dirty we might say, 'You're **as** black **as** coal!'
  Use these words to complete the phrases below:

peacock	honey	snow	fox	lemon	nails	feather	dove
houses	pin	lion	ice	pancake	tomato		

as cold as _____ as brave as a _____

as clever as a _____ as flat as a _____

as gentle as a _____ as hard as _____

as light as a _____ as safe as _____

as proud as a _____ as red as a _____

as sharp as a _____ as sour as _____

as sweet as _____ as white as _____

Make up your own similes – choose something no-one has ever heard of before!

as purple as _____ as squashy as a _____

as wriggly as _____ as loud as _____

- My bed is **as comfortable as** _____
     (What is the softest thing you can think of?)
- The dustbin smell was **as bad as** _____
     (What is the worst smell you can think of?)
- The film was **as frightening as** _____
     (What scares you most?)

RC6 (Activity 2) Similes

What do you think it means?

1. Roger is **as tall as a lamppost**.
   - a. He is a lamppost.
   - b. He is very tall.
   - c. He likes lampposts.
2. Dad has a face **like thunder**.
   - a. He was wet.
   - b. He was dirty.
   - c. He was cross.
3. Gran's hair was **like a bird's nest**.
   - a. She forgot to brush her hair.
   - b. She had a hat on with feathers in it.
   - c. She had a parrot at home.
4. The baby hamster was **as wriggly as a worm**.
   - a. The hamster was a worm.
   - b. The hamster wriggled and escaped.
   - c. The hamster was difficult to hold.
5. The policeman is **as strong as a horse**.
   - a. The policeman can pull carts like a horse.
   - b. The policeman is on a horse.
   - c. The policeman can lift heavy things.
6. Her face is **as red as beetroot**.
   - a. She has been eating beetroot.
   - b. She is looking hot.
   - c. She has got beetroot juice on her face.
7. All the children were **as good as gold**.
   - a. They were worth a lot of money.
   - b. They were behaving well.
   - c. They wore gold clothes.
8. I am **as warm as toast**.
   - a. I want to eat some toast.
   - b. I put my hand in the toaster.
   - c. I feel nice and cosy.
9. Susan's head was as hot **as fire**.
   - a. She had burnt her head.
   - b. She was ill and had a temperature.
   - c. Her hair was on fire.
10. My school bag is **as heavy as lead**.
    - a. It is full of books.
    - b. Someone has put lead in the bottom.
    - c. It is made of metal.
11. The witch's hands were **like claws**.
    - a. She was holding a bird.
    - b. She had claws instead of fingers.
    - c. Her fingers were bent and spiky.
12. The soldier stood **as stiff as a poker**.
    - a. He was poking someone.

b. He was feeling stiff.

c. He stood very straight.

13. The boy felt **as fit as a flea**.

 a. He feels lively.

 b. He has got fleas.

 c. He can jump very high.

14. The footballer is **as keen as mustard**.

 a. He wants to win very much.

 b. He likes mustard.

 c. He puts mustard on his football.

15. My little brother is **as happy as a sandboy**.

 a. He likes to play in the sand.

 b. He is very happy.

 c. He wants a job as a sandboy.

RC7 Metaphors

Metaphors are like similes but they say or suggest one thing **is** another rather than **like** another.

Some are likely to be heard in spoken language, such as:

He's **a big pussycat**.
The man **is a tiger** when he fights.
My feet **are blocks of ice**.

The child who does not understand metaphors will be confused if he takes the statements literally. He needs encouraging to ask so that the confusion can be cleared up. In order to understand properly the child needs to be able to recognise attributes of people, place and objects. He then needs to be able to understand similes. Only then is he likely to understand that metaphors are like similes without the **like** or **as**.

Most metaphors are encountered in imaginative and poetic writing. Creating a metaphor is a fairly sophisticated operation, so it should not be expected in children who have not mastered the less sophisticated figures of speech, such as similes and attributions. Examples of literary metaphors include:

A white blanket of snow covered the ground.
The mountains **tumbled** down to the sea.
The factory chimney sent **snakes** of grey into the sky.

Until he is ready, the child needs to recognise his own confusion and ask.

RC8 Inference

Inference is when the meaning of something is obtained from more than just pieces of information presented in sequence. It requires making a connection between the pieces of information and then going beyond it to make another meaning. For instance, a child might be told, or read,

'Help!' shouted Sam. There was a splash.

To understand this, the child has to connect the **help!** with the **splash**, and make a hypothesis that Sam has fallen into some water. Sometimes a child will make this connection but have a fixed idea that, for instance, it must be at the seaside because that is where he has seen someone fall over and make a splash. He will then tend to ignore the next piece of information, **Susan ran to the bank**, because it does not fit with what he expects.

These children need encouraging to make connections to make a hypothesis, but then need to be willing to change this in the light of fresh information. They need encouraging to check their conclusions against their common sense.

When supporting a child who can recall information literally you need to question him about what he has heard, and point out that there is a connection; encourage him to guess, then to change this if necessary. To do this, he needs to feel safe and that it is all right to make a wrong hypothesis. Emphasise that there is no such thing as failure, only feedback.

Using written language can be helpful for a child who can read because writing is not ephemeral and the child can take as long as he needs to work out connections. This resolves difficulties with auditory memory.

It can be helpful, if it is appropriate and there is time, to practise using inference as a skill on specially structured activities (see pp.51–54).

RC9 Activity: Simple predictions

Say, 'What will happen if . . .?'

1. You pull the cat's tail.
2. You pour water into a paper bag.
3. You touch a hot cooker.
4. You cut your finger.
5. Your dog sees a cat.
6. You try to rollerblade on grass.
7. The roof leaks.
8. You forget your PE kit.
9. You throw a stone at a window.
10. You drop a glass on a hard floor.
11. You write on the wall with felt tip pen.
12. You spill juice on the carpet.
13. You put the plug in the bath and leave the tap running.
14. You don't put the ice-cream in the freezer.
15. You plant some seeds but forget to water them.
16. You kick a ball hard with your bare foot.
17. You walk through a puddle in your shoes.
18. You play in the snow without your gloves.
19. You put money in a pocket with a hole in.
20. You walk on a drawing pin when you've only got socks on.
21. Your mother forgets to take the cake out of the oven.
22. You let go of a balloon in the shopping centre.
23. The electricity goes off in your house.
24. You forget to take your coat to school.
25. You run into a busy road without looking.

RC10 Activity: If . . . then

Ask the child to complete these sentences:

1. **If** your hands are dirty, **then** . . .
2. **If** you jump into a swimming pool , **then** . . .
3. **If** your shoes are too small, **then** . . .
4. **If** your tooth is loose, **then** . . .
5. **If** you find a purse, **then** . . .
6. **If** your pencil gets blunt, **then** . . .
7. **If** you eat too much, **then** . . .
8. **If** you have a hole in your sock, **then** . . .
9. **If** you have a runny nose, **then** . . .
10. **If** you don't do your homework, **then** . . .
11. **If** you unplug the fridge, **then** . . .
12. **If** you want your friends to come, **then** . . .
13. **If** your hair is too long, **then** . . .
14. **If** the tyre on your bike is flat, **then** . . .
15. **If** it is your mum's birthday tomorrow, **then** . . .
16. **If** the dog has a sore leg, **then** . . .
17. **If** the telephone rings, **then** . . .
18. **If** it is cold outside, **then** . . .
19. **If** someone says hello to you, **then** . . .
20. **If** your TV breaks down, **then** . . .
21. **If** you are tired, **then** . . .

RC11 Deductions

Children can be asked simple questions involving deduction, such as:

- What is round and found on a car?
- What opens and shuts?
- What do people keep their money in?
- What can take people up and down in a big shop?
- What can you use to make yourself clean?

This can be developed into a 'What am I?' game. The child has to say what the object is after being given a series of clues. For example:

1. I can fly. I have soft feathers.
2. I can fly. I have pretty wings.
3. I can swim. I am shiny and slippery.
4. I can swim. I am black. I will grow into a frog.
5. I am in the sky. I am round. I make you hot.
6. I can be eaten. I am white or brown. I have a shell.
7. I am an animal. I live with people. I have a collar. I can bark.
8. I am part of a house. I break easily. I have a frame. I let the light in.
9. I am round and crisp. I grow on a tree. You eat me.
10. I have four legs. I have a flat top. You eat your meals off me.
11. I have a handle. You can open and close me. I keep your head dry.
12. You have two of me. They have nails. They can hold things.
13. I am made of metal. You carry me about. I like to open things.
14. I am orange. I grow in the ground. Rabbits like to eat me.
15. I am green. You cut me down in winter. You like to decorate me.

Children can be encouraged to make up their own definitions, of, for example, a chair/clock/bird/book and ask others to guess what they are. This formula can be adapted to, 'Who am I?' Use nursery rhyme characters, cartoon characters etc. Again, the children can ask others to guess. Examples are:

1. I sat on some grass. I was going to eat. A spider frightened me away.
2. I went to see my grandma. I walked through the wood. I met a wolf.
3. I look after animals. They got lost. They came home wagging their tails.
4. I went up a hill with my sister. We went for water. I fell down and hurt my head.

RC12 Cloze and connections

This is a technique that involves omitting words in a text so that the pupil has to 'fill the gap' with a word that makes sense. To do this, he has to draw on his knowledge of sentence grammar and vocabulary and his awareness of context.

Cloze texts are useful to help children practise their skills in connecting information given in writing. They also learn that cues to complete the cloze texts can work forwards as well as backwards.

There are many books containing cloze texts on the market. However, ordinary texts can be made and target words deleted. Make sure there is enough information either before or after the deletion to give sufficient cues for the child to complete the text.

Here is an example.

Pets

The people of Rolf Street have strange (1) _____. Mr Smith, in number one, has a green (2) _____. His next door neighbour, in number (3) _____, complains about the noise. She doesn't like to (4) _____ swearing and squawking when she sits in the (5) _____ on sunny days. Over the road, the people in number two (6) _____ to keep ferrets. These fierce (7) _____ were kept in a hutch. Then they (8) _____. No-one found them, but Miss Lane, from two doors down, was very (9) _____. Her (10) _____ came in from the garden with a bitten ear. The poodle from number (11) _____ will never win a prize in a dog (12) _____ again.

Cues the child needs to use to complete this text:

1. **pets** – reference to the title and the subjects referred to throughout.
2. **parrot** – cues for this in next two sentences: 'noise', 'swearing', 'squawking'.
3. **three** – cues for this: next door to number one, street numbering pattern.
4. **hear** – cue: 'noise'.
5. **garden** – cues: 'sit', 'sunny day', where she would hear the parrot.
6. **used** – cue in next sentence, 'were kept'.
7. **animals** – cue: 'ferrets' in previous sentence.
8. **escaped** – cue: 'no-one found them' in the next sentence.
9. **upset** – cues in next two sentences.
10. **dog** – cues in next two sentences.
11. **five** – cue: two doors from number one.
12. **show** – cue: 'prize'.

RC13 Between the lines

1. Hedgehogs have lots of fleas. They can't lick themselves clean. **Why?**
2. Mrs Smith heard a squeal of brakes, then a scream. **What do you think had happened?**
3. After the storm, Tom and Neil went for a walk on the beach. They found an oar and some pieces of smashed, curved wood. **What might have happened?**
4. The slaves were getting desperate. They had to arrange to meet in a cave. **Why?**
5. Louise had a mark on her new shoes. Fortunately, she had some Tippex with her. **What colour were her shoes?**
6. Tom and Ben ran up and down the beach. It was cold. Tom's teeth chattered. Ben's ears flapped. **What can you tell about Tom and Ben?**
7. It was dark and very foggy. The boat crashed onto the rocks. **What could they *not* see?**
8. It was December. It was getting dark and Ian felt hungry. **What time would it say if he had a watch?**
9. It was June. It was getting dark and Ian felt sleepy. **What time would it say on his watch?**
10. Mark got on the bus. Unfortunately, he had left his wallet at home. **Did he get to work on time?**
11. After dinner, Danny's mother said, 'It's your turn.' Danny started with the cleanest things and did the dirtiest things at the end. **What was he doing?**
12. Amy was pleased with her birthday present. She sorted the pieces into two groups, depending on their shape. Then she did the edges and filled in the middle later. **What was she doing?**
13. Mr Robson sorted the things into piles, depending on their colour and material. He knew if he put them in at the wrong temperature they might be ruined. **What was he doing?**
14. It was Jack's mother's birthday soon. He put an advertisement in the local shop to say he had some rollerblades for sale. **Why?**
15. During the war, I worked on a battleship. When we were on battle alert we slept in our clothes. **Why?** The laundry service was not very busy during battle alert. **Why?** Every two or three days a helicopter arrived with the mail. Then silence fell over the ship. **Why?**

RC14 Comprehension: IEP targets

These should be **S**pecific, **M**easurable, **A**chievable, **R**elevant, **T**imed (i.e. **SMART**)
Choose the most appropriate from the list below:

- **recognise the purpose of lies/white lies/irony/persuasion** – *see RC3* (pp.38–39)
- **recognise and understand figures of speech** – *see RC4* (p.40) *and RC8* (pp.49–50)
- **recognise attributes/classify by attributes** – *see RC5* (pp.41–44)
- **recognise and make similes** – *see RC6* (pp.45–47)
- **recognise and create metaphors** – *see RC7* (p.48)
- **make simple predictions** – *see RC10* (p.51) *and RC11* (p.52)
- **make deductions/inferences based on verbal/textual information**
  – (*see RC9* (p.50), *RC12* (p.53), *and RC13* (p.54)

(*specify*)
with adult support/independently

2 Non-verbal difficulties

ATTENTION AND LISTENING

AL1 Early listening

If the child is easily distracted, ensure you are in a quiet room or corner which is comparatively free of interesting things other than those to be used. If the child does not already know you, allow time for him to gain some confidence and to become interested and willing to cooperate. Make a game of each situation, building on what the child CAN do, and making use of his interests. Always ensure that you have the child's attention and that he understands what is required of him.

Some ideas for games to develop early listening skills

- The 'Go' game. Use a simple stacking toy or jigsaw. The child can place one piece at a time after the word 'go'.
- The 'Give me' game. Put out an array of several objects. Say 'Give me a . . .' (variations: 'Show me a . . .', 'Touch a . . .').
- Any version of the 'O'Grady' or 'Simon Says' games.
- Perform appropriate actions to any familiar songs and rhymes.
- Acting out short well-known stories.
- Identify household and familiar sounds using real objects, e.g. spoon rattling in a cup, paper rustling, pouring water.
- Match animal sounds with toy farm animals.
- Tell a story, allowing time for the child to make the correct sounds in the appropriate place. This can be done in a group with each child having a different sound, e.g. animals, wind, footsteps, knocking.
- Identify all kinds of sounds on tape. Initially match these with real objects, if possible, then progress to matching sounds to pictures.
- Use a tape of sounds, with sets of pictures to play 'Sound Lotto'.
- Make two identical sets of 'sound boxes', e.g. film canisters containing rice, sugar, counters etc. All the containers should look alike. The child has to match the pairs by sound.
- Identify familiar voices on tape.
- Follow simple instructions, starting individually, e.g. 'stand on one leg'. Then work in groups: 'blue group, touch your ears'.
- In pairs, one child instructs another to draw a picture, or colour in a picture. A screen should be used between the children.

- Tapping patterns. Tap a pattern on the table which the child has to match. Start with a simple tap-tap-tap and work up to more complex patterns as the child shows progress.
- Musical tones. Fill three glasses or bottles with unequal amounts of water. Tap a tone pattern (e.g. high, low, middle) for the child to copy. Start off with simple patterns, then introduce more difficult ones. At first, the child listens and looks at the pattern being made. Later, he should copy the pattern just by listening. This can be varied to include loud and quiet tones as well as long and short tones. (He can also be encouraged to remember and use this sort of vocabulary.)
- Classifying non-verbal sounds. Using a taped or imitated sound, ask the child to classify sounds as to whether they are: (a) mechanical/non-mechanical (b) loud/quiet (c) friendly/unfriendly animals.
- Classifying spoken words. Name objects – the child classifies according to whether they are: (a) long/short words (e.g. astronaut/cat) (b) long/short sentences.

AL2 Early listening activities

If the child is easily distracted, ensure you are in a quiet room or corner which is comparatively free of interesting things other than those to be used. If the child does not already know you, allow time for him to gain some confidence and to become interested and willing to cooperate. Make a game of each situation, building on what the child CAN do, and making use of his interests. Always ensure that you have the child's attention and that he understands what is required of him.

Some ideas for games to develop early listening skills

- Listen for a 'cue' word. The child puts a counter in a pot when he hears the cue word (which can be varied) in a story. This can be done with a group.
- Listen for a particular sound in words, e.g. 's'. The child can put a counter in a pot (or similar reward) for the correct response.
- Spot deliberate mistakes either in 'silly sentences', e.g. 'We had grass for our dinner', or in familiar rhymes, sounds or stories.
- Complete a sentence, e.g. 'I put my shoes on and . . .' Accept any reply that makes sense.
- In a group/pairs, make up a story. Each child adds one sentence in turn (a sort of verbal 'Consequences').
- Discriminate between real words/nonsense words – in a list, in a passage.
- The child says 'same'/'not the same' for pairs of words (real and nonsense) spoken to him, e.g. man/nan, pit/bit, pot/top, noss/noss, gatt/datt.
- Give the child a short sentence and ask him to say a little bit of it, e.g. 'The cat is naughty.'

AL3 Overcoming passive listening

Some children find listening difficult. This may be because they have general or specific comprehension difficulties, they process language slowly, or have attention or hearing difficulties.

Children with long-standing comprehension difficulties become used to being confused. They tend to guess at answers or attempt to change the subject so that they are not in a failing situation. They expect to be wrong and to be corrected, and have become passive listeners.

These children need to learn:

- the rules of good listening
- that although they do not understand, it is not necessarily their fault – it can be the fault of the speaker who has not been sufficiently aware of the needs of the child
- that although it may not be their fault it **is** their responsibility to say that they do not understand
- to ask for clarification by identifying the reason for not understanding, and/or the part of the message which is not understood
- to ask the speaker to make the message clear with an appropriate comment or question about all or part of the message.

AL4 Rules for good listening

Children with listening and comprehension difficulties need to know that **not speaking** does not mean they are automatically **listening**!

They need to know what good listening is. They need to know the rules, and why, for example, looking at the speaker helps to keep their mind on the same subject. The rules can be displayed in the classroom in written or pictorial form.

The rules of good listening

- Sit still.
- Look at the speaker.
- Think about the words.

These rules can probably be best understood through role play, so another adult will be needed. It is only when children have recognised the behaviour in others that they will recognise it in themselves and be able to change it.

Role play

While the teacher speaks, the other adult could:

- look out of the window (not looking at the speaker)
- fidget, twiddle pencils (not sitting still)
- answer incorrectly (not listening to the words).

Encourage the children to say what is wrong, e.g. 'not looking', 'not thinking'.

Give clear feedback, praise good behaviour and correct in a neutral voice. Sample comments would be:

- I can see Lisa is looking hard at Mrs Brown, and thinking. Good listening, Lisa!
- You sat very still, Ross, and that was good. But you didn't look at me. Let's try again.
- You gave me a good answer. Good listening!
- Sit still Martha, and look at me. Now, that's much better listening!
- Look at Michael. He's sitting still and looking at Miss Smith. He's learned to be a good listener.

AL5 Clarification and active listening

Asking for clarification

This can only happen when a child has recognised that he has not understood a spoken message, whether it is a request, question or explanation.

Children need to know why messages break down. Role play with another adult can be useful to show examples of breakdown, encouraging the children to recognise and say what went wrong and how they can ask for help. The most effective questions and comments may need to be modelled.

Examples

- **The teacher speaks too quickly.**
  'Slow down, please.'
- **The teacher speaks too quietly.**
  'Could you say it louder, please.'
- **There is too much other noise.**
  'I couldn't hear that because Michael was coughing/the others were talking/the TV was too loud' etc.
- **The message is impossible.**
  'But you haven't given me the pencil.'
  'You said give this to Emma and she isn't here today.'
  'I haven't got a partner.'
- **The message is unclear.**
  'Which book do I need?'
  'Which Richard do you mean?'
- **The message is too difficult.**
  'I don't understand.'
- **The message is too long.**
  'I can't remember all that.'
  'I can't remember the first bit.'
- **The message contains difficult vocabulary.**
  'I don't know what orbit means.'
  'Does cooperation mean the same as helping?'
- **The sentence grammar is too difficult.**
  'Is it the boy who chases the ball or the dog?'
  'What do you mean?'

You can help a child identify difficulties by asking questions such as:

- 'Did I say that too fast?'
- 'Was there a word you didn't understand?'
- 'Would you like me to say that again?'

Listening can also be made more active by:

- Giving a reason for listening beforehand, for example, so the child will be able to carry out a particular activity afterwards:
  'Listen so you will be able to make your own box afterwards.'

- Introducing new vocabulary and names beforehand, for example:

  'We are going to find out which materials are good conductors today. Remind me what a conductor is.'

  'This story is about a boy called Sam and a dog call Barney. What's the boy's name? What do we call the dog?'

- Giving a synopsis of what is to come, for example:

  'This is an account of what happened to a little girl in the last war, and how she came to die.'

- Providing a context for what is to come, for example:

  'The Second World War was how many years ago? Was your father or your grandfather in it? How old was he at the beginning of the war?'

  'Remember that both these families have been at war for a hundred years. This boy has grown up used to seeing tanks in the streets.'

Ask the child to repeat what he thinks he has heard as soon as possible after the instruction. Questions to ask might be:

- 'What have you got to do?' (describe the task)
- 'What have you got to do first/next . . .' etc. (describe the sequence)
- 'Why do you have to do this?' (describe the purpose)
- 'How will you know when you have finished?' (describe the expected result)

AL6 Classroom strategies to help poor listeners

Carpet time

- Give the child a special place to sit (near the teacher or other adult), and give him lots of eye contact or gentle touches to remind him of the rules of good listening.
- Give the child something to hold for you, e.g. word cards or a book, to stop him fidgeting. He is more likely to listen better in order to give the cards etc. at the right time.
- Include the child's name in passing, such as, 'James, you've got a cat at home, haven't you?' or whatever fits in with the topic being discussed.

General strategies

- Sit the child near the front and make frequent eye contact.
- Gain the child's attention before making an announcement, by using his name or tapping the board.
- During instruction, regain the child's attention by casually mentioning his name.
- Don't sit the pupil near classroom distractions such as heaters, doors, windows, noisy areas and well-used pathways.
- Visual support such as flash cards and pictures to instructions and explanations will aid attention.
- Keep instructions as short as possible. Break into small steps, and when one has been completed, move on to another. Try to ensure that the child has a sense of accomplishment.
- Ensure the pupil understands the task. If there appears to be confusion, be careful to distinguish between misbehaviour and misunderstanding.

AL7 Following instructions

Some children have difficulties responding to verbal instructions, especially in a group or class situation, because:

- they cannot cope with instructions given to the whole group – they may not perceive themselves as one of the group and that the instruction is meant for them as well as others
- the language used for giving instructions may be too long or complex
- poor listening and attention and awareness of what other children are doing exacerbate the difficulty of following instructions.

Ideas to try

- Repeat group instructions individually to the child:
  - preface instruction with the child's name to focus attention (other group members may also benefit from an opportunity of hearing the instruction again)
  - use the Learning Support Assistant to repeat the instruction (but do not reword it or the child may think it is a different instruction)
  - use peers to repeat instruction.
- Simplify language by making sentences:
  - shorter
  - simpler.
- Give only one instruction at a time, especially if it is part of a series of instructions.
- Use visual aids such as objects, pictures and diagrams to aid understanding.
- Encourage the child to observe and copy what other children are doing.
- Teach the child to seek clarification if the instruction is not understood.

AL8 Encouraging independent working

Some children have difficulty working independently. The child may not know:

- whether the work is to be done on his own or with others
- where he should be for what activity
- what he is supposed to do and how he will know when he is finished
- what he is supposed to do when he is finished
- what he should do if he needs help.

These children can be helped by having a calm and ordered classroom with:

- Labelled work areas within the classroom, such as the book corner, the painting area (this helps the child be aware of boundaries).
- Clearly labelled equipment.
- A daily schedule, listing daily tasks and activities (this can be done with words or symbols).
- A weekly timetable or planner using words or symbols to help the child gain some understanding of time and be better prepared for changes.
- Prompt cards with visual instructions (pictures, symbols, photos or simple phrases) which can be displayed clearly or carried around so the child knows what is expected of him. These cards could show:
  - where the child should be
  - what activity he should be doing
  - when to listen
  - when he can talk
  - who chooses the activity – teacher or child.

The card can be returned to a special box at the end of the appropriate period and a new one selected.

- Work areas on a table or a sitting space on the carpet marked out by sticky tape. This also helps prevent intrusion into another child's personal space.
- A work station where the child can be instructed or can work on his own without distractions.

AL9 Managing children with attention and concentration difficulties

General considerations

- Make sure all staff involved take a consistent approach. A whole-school approach involves teaching and non-teaching staff and includes all areas (including corridors and playgrounds).
- Frequent liaison with parents is desirable, for instance by using a home/school book to liaise on positive aspects as well as negative. This will avoid a crisis management style of communication.
- Pupils with concentration and attention problems have difficulty staying in control so:
  - remain calm
  - be consistent
  - do not get into debates or arguments.
- Try to be consistent. Do not ignore a behaviour one day when you may challenge it on another.
- Do not reprimand the child in public. It is not an effective way of managing behaviour because it draws attention to the bad behaviour and distracts other pupils.
- You can't make a child behave. He is more likely to behave if he feels you genuinely care about him and will listen to him even if you do not agree with him.
- Be fair. This means doing the right thing for each child, which is not necessarily the same thing for everyone.

Management in the classroom

- Be clear about rules, rewards and consequences. Display these in a prominent position for all to see and refer to them frequently.
- Avoid sitting the child near distractions such as heaters, doors, windows, noisy areas and well-used pathways.
- Have a special quiet area for any pupil who needs a quiet place to work.
- Make frequent eye contact with the child and sit him near the front.
- Regain the pupil's attention in class discussions by casually or incidentally mentioning his name.
- Gain the child's attention before making an announcement by using his name or tapping on the board.
- Keep routines predictable. If a change is unavoidable give extra explanation and time for the child to accept this. Wherever possible, prepare in advance.
- Prepare for tasks, for example by having a pencil box ready. Simplify choices. Encourage self-monitoring, e.g. use of timer if this is not a distraction.
- Consider alternatives to copious hand-written tasks, such as using information technology (IT) or multi-choice answers, breakthrough cards, cloze texts etc.
- Teach the whole class the rules of good listening and display rules. These are:
  - sit still
  - look at the speaker
  - think about the words.

Teacher–pupil agreement and interaction

- Encourage positive self-talk and self-monitoring by the pupil.
- Develop a prompt or cue with the child for when he goes off task to return him to work.
- Watch for 'meltdown'. Prior agreement of strategies and procedures, which may include 'time out', to be followed consistently and may be built into class rules.
- Praise/reward acceptable/appropriate behaviour generously and consistently. This helps the pupil be aware of the behaviour you want rather than the behaviour you don't want.
- Teach the desirable behaviour. Be specific, such as, 'Look at the person who is talking, put up your hand if you want to say something, then wait until you are called before you talk', rather than, 'Don't interrupt.'
- The child must be involved if behaviour is to improve. Let the child know you know how hard it is for him when _____ but that you want to work with him to improve _____. Agree one behaviour with the pupil (like staying in his seat throughout a task and help him to work out ways that will achieve this).
- Help the child to focus on strategies that he thinks will help him succeed (such as seating, other child, visual prompts etc.).
- Encourage self-monitoring by asking questions such as, 'Do you know what you just said?', 'Why do you think Tom looked sad when you said that?'
- Agree jointly the amount of time in which to complete a task. Gradually encourage him to set his own time targets.
- Encourage the child to take increasing responsibility, for instance by remembering particular equipment. Help him choose a structure to aid him such as:
  - a weekly chart, to remember PE kit etc.
  - daily routine chart, with visual or word prompts
  - visual prompt for task on hand.

Other strategies

- Break down instructions, directions etc. into small parts. Too much given at one time will cause an overload. The child may need more repetitions and reminders than other children. Any visual support to information/instruction given verbally will aid attention.
- Expect quality rather than quantity. Set realistic tasks that take poor concentration span into account. Eliminate or reduce timed tasks and break big tasks into smaller parts.
- If the child shows moments of creativity or talent, acknowledge it and encourage the rest of the class to see it too.
- Give him recognition of good behaviour.
- Set limits. Keep instructions and explanations short, simple and to the point and take control. For example, 'Sit down here' **not** 'Would you like to sit here?'
- Be careful to distinguish between misbehaviour and misunderstanding.
- Encourage awareness of non-verbal cues and body language through role play and drama.
- Try to end interactions with all pupils in a positive way.
- Try to ensure periods of vigorous exercise in each day. This helps to break up physical and emotional tensions and reduce stress.

AL10 Attention and listening: IEP targets

These should be Specific, Measurable, Achievable, Relevant, Timed (i.e. **SMART**). Choose the most appropriate from the list below:

- **identify familiar sounds/link sounds to pictures** – *see AL1* (pp.56–57)
- **respond to one-word/short instructions** – *see AL1* (pp.56–57)
- **copy simple rhythm patterns** – *see AL1* (pp.56–57)
- **listen and respond correctly to cue words** – *see AL2* (p.58)
- **discriminate between sounds in nonsense/real words** – *see AL2* (p.58)
- **repeat/complete short sentences** – *seeAL2* (p.58)
- **sit still and look at the speaker** (*specify for how long, and where, e.g. carpet time – see AL3* (p.59) *and AL4* (p.60))
- **repeat what he thinks has been said** – *see AL5* (p.61–62)
- **say when he has not understood/and recognise the reason for the breakdown** (*see AL5* (pp.61–62))
- **know and say what he has to do/where he should do it/how he knows he has finished/what to do when finished** – *see AL6* (p.63) *and AL8* (p.65)
- **know when he can/can't speak** – *see AL8* (p.65)
- **know which areas are out of bounds** – *see AL8* (p.65)
- **stay on task for agreed length of time** (*specify what, where, how long – see AL8* (p.65) *and AL9* (pp.66–67))
- **use strategies/prompts agreed beforehand to help return to task** – *see AL9* (pp.66–67)

(*specify*)
with adult support/within a small group/within the whole class/independently.

AUDITORY MEMORY
AM1 Developing auditory memory skills

There are three different types of memory:

- immediate recall (**short-term memory**)
- retention of information while processing and acting on it (**working memory**)
- storage of information for future use (**long-term memory**).

Some children find it hard to remember all of what they hear. Their ability to recall what they have heard, in the right order, and retain the information long enough for it to be processed and acted upon is seriously affected. They may have a poor short-term memory or difficulty in storing information in their long-term memory, and consequently need information to be repeated more often than other children.

Listening entails remembering things in order. Some children rely on visual memory, or their memory of experiences. They can remember what they have seen and what they have done but not things they are told, in the right order.

Rote memory requires no comprehension whereas verbal comprehension requires understanding. A normal person may only be able to recall and repeat six or seven random words or numbers in a sequence, but may accurately remember a sentence of more than 20 words, because it has meaning.

Children with poor auditory memory can only retain a few ideas or key words at any one time. Research has shown that a child's memory span can be improved, but after about age eight improvement seems to stop. However, verbal memory can continue to improve as the child's understanding grows. This is done by helping the children to 'organise' how they remember things and use strategies such as visualising and cueing to compensate for their difficulties.

It is usually better to encourage children not to guess, but to say, 'I forgot what you said,' rather than guess and misunderstand.

Ideas for developing a child's memory span

- 'Listen to me' sequence. Use coloured beads, toys, crayons. Instruct the child to place the objects in order, e.g. red, yellow, blue. Always make sure the child listens to the end of the instruction and repeats it correctly before carrying out the sequence.
- Variations of 'I went to market', e.g. 'I went on holiday and took/saw a . . .' – each child should add one more item and repeat the string.
- Carrying messages. Increase the number of items to be remembered.
- 'Telephone number' game (a toy telephone can be used). The adult says a number (start with three numbers) and the child has to dial/repeat the number.
- Give a string of very simple instructions for the child to follow, e.g. touch the wall/then stand on the chair. Increase the length of the string of instructions.

AM2 Key Stage 1 auditory memory intervention strategies

- Always encourage **left to right** sequencing.
- Work on games to **increase memory span**.
- When giving class instructions, **check recall** by asking the child to tell the adult what he has to do before carrying it out.
- It may be helpful to have some sort of **picture** or **symbol** for the child to take with him to remind him of what is to be done.
- In circle time, the children can be asked to **remember another child's news**. At first the child should know whose news he has to remember, and tell it immediately. Later, include one or two other children's news in between.
- Give a small group of children a single, different command each, then see if they can **remember everyone else's** – not their own.
- New material needs to be presented **visually** as well as auditorily.
- **Present the 'big' picture first**, then the details. This gives the opportunity to elaborate on what is being learned.

Adults should:

- use prompts/pictures/symbols
- 'chunk' information – pause between bits of information so the chunks are short and meaningful, e.g. 'go to the bottom of the page/and draw a circle around/the jar with the most sweets'. This way the child has time to absorb/visualise and act on before hearing the next chunk.

The child should be encouraged to:

- 'chunk' – pick out three words/ideas they have to remember
- rehearse – repeat key words only, then repeat sequence if relevant.

In general, it is better to give the child a specific purpose for listening before the activity. What doesn't work:

- **pressure**
- **working to time limits**
- **over-stimulation.**

AM3 Key Stage 2 auditory memory intervention strategies

- **Encourage clarification** – 'Can you say the last bit again, please?'
- **Introduce delays between giving an instruction and the child carrying it out** – to the end of the lesson/day/next week.
- **Encourage visualisation techniques**. Let the child imagine himself doing the actions – really see it in his head. Make comical connections between pieces of information, items in a list etc.
- **Mnemonics** – let children make up their own to help them learn sequences such as the planets in the solar system.
- **Practise programming a video**. After a while, the child should be able to remember longer sequences of numbers.
- **Play telephone message games** – an adult pretends to phone and the child has to take the message. He needs to recognise key points within a normal stream of conversation. He can write/draw/use symbols to convey message, e.g. Get Gran/station/9.15 pm.
- **Encourage word relationships**, such as 'Which word doesn't belong?', 'How are these the same/different?'
- **Play verbal absurdities**, e.g. say why the sentence *doesn't* make sense.
- **Play deduction games**. 'What am I?' The child is given three clues to deduce the answer, for example, 'I have four legs. I am often made of wood. You sit on me.'
- **Use stories demanding inference**, where the child has to supply information from his experience, e.g. 'There was a loud bang and glass in the road. What had happened?'

AM4 Auditory memory: IEP targets

These should be **S**pecific, **M**easurable, **A**chievable, **R**elevant, **T**imed (i.e. **SM**A
 Choose the most appropriate from the list below:

- **repeat a sequence of two/three/four/five items in order from verbal instruction** –
 see AM1 (p.69)
- **remember a sequence of words within a group game** – *see AM1* (p.69), *AM2* (p.70)
 and AM3 (p.71)
- **repeat simple instructions containing two/three/four/five 'bits' of information** –
 see AM1, AM2 and AM3 (pp.69–71)

(*specify*)
with adult support/within a small group/within the whole class/independently.

3 Expressive language difficulties

E1 Expressive language difficulties

Children can have difficulty expressing themselves for three main reasons.

1. They may have word-finding difficulties. This means that the child uses a small vocabulary of frequently used words and often cannot **say** precisely what he has no difficulty **understanding**. He has to use other words as substitutes, such as 'play on' or 'sit on' the horse rather than 'ride' the horse. There will be a high number of non-specific words such as 'get', 'put', or 'thingy'. Some children can explain themselves another way while others break down and cannot go on. This often relates to auditory memory difficulties. For ideas and strategies to help, see the EV section.
2. The grammar they are able to use is immature even when they can understand other people's sentence grammar perfectly well. There is an order to the development of sentence grammar. For instance, the child will say 'I' and 'me' before using 'myself', and 'doggy run' before 'the dog is running'. For ideas on strategies to help develop sentence grammar, see the EG section.
3. Some children have difficulty producing mature speech sounds, in which case they are likely to be seeing a speech and language therapist. These difficulties usually mean that the child's phonological system – the system by which the child can recognise and reproduce individual sounds in clusters (such as 'sk') and sequences (such as east/eats) – is delayed or disordered. The same difficulties mean that the child is likely to have problems acquiring phonic skills at the usual age, with likely literacy difficulties – in particular with spelling. In their early years, these children will need specialist support. Advice on how to manage unintelligible children is given in section S. Advice is also given in this section on how to manage children who stammer, and those who rarely speak in school.

Some children do not use their language for a range of purposes appropriate to their age, especially when there have been any of the above difficulties, although this is not inevitably the case. When none of the above difficulties are present there could be general learning difficulties or the child may have an autistic spectrum disorder. See section UL for ideas to help.

Finally, some children have poor conversation skills, usually referred to as 'pragmatic' difficulties. Often, although not always, there may be poor social interaction skills as well. Children on the autistic spectrum have poor conversation skills. For advice, see Conversation Skills pp.108–119.

EXPRESSIVE VOCABULARY

EV1 Word finding

Some children have difficulties retrieving and using words they know. These children often have a poor memory for sounds and may need to hear a word many times before they can remember it well enough to use. They may need to be encouraged to repeat it several times on several occasions before it is well enough learned.

You can often tell a child has a word-finding difficulty if he uses a high number of non-specific words, such as 'get', 'put', 'that', or says 'you know' or 'thingy'. Some children will use another similar word – such as 'worm' for 'snake', 'kite' for 'parachute', 'horse' for 'camel' – even when they know it is wrong.

To help a child remember a word well enough he needs to learn it well. The more ways a word can be linked to other words and meanings to help retrieval at a later date, the better. One way to help the child learn a word well in the first place is by helping him to understand what type of thing it represents, e.g. furniture, weather, feelings etc. – in other words, what **category** of words this word belongs to.

- Describe an object. Give the child a picture and ask him to describe it to you or another child. You can help him by giving sentences to complete, such as 'It has . . .', 'It looks like . . .', 'It is for . . .', 'You can find/see/play with it at . . .', etc.
- Definitions. The child can guess the word from a given definition, such as, 'It is orange. It grows in the ground. You can eat it.' Children can play these games in teams – one team giving definitions or acting them out, the other guessing the word.
- Always encourage the child to 'find' the specific word rather than use non-specific words, even though this may take time. He may need to 'talk round' a specific word he cannot remember.

There are two main strategies to help a child recall a word he has forgotten. Some children respond much better than others to one or other strategy.

Phonological cueing

This involves children responding to sounds in a word. They can be asked, and then, in time, ask themselves:

- Is it a long or short word?
- What sound does it begin with?
- Can you think of any other sounds in the word, not just the first sound?
- Can you find a real or made-up word to rhyme with it?
- Can you clap how many syllables it has?

Semantic cueing

This involves children responding to the meanings of words, and how it is associated to other meanings. The child can be asked, and eventually ask himself:

- What sort of a group does this word belong to? (**category**)
- What does it do? (**function**)
- Where might you find it? (**context**)
- Can you describe it? (**description**)
- What else is this like? (for a noun) (**similarity**)
  or
  What else can you do like this? (for a verb)
- What else does it make you think of? (**association**)

EV2 'Empty' words

A child may make use of too many 'empty' or non-specific words, such as 'get', 'put' or 'thing'. This may be because:

- he has a word-finding difficulty
- he does not know that there is a word which expresses his meaning more accurately
- he is reluctant to use the words he knows and understands.

In the case of a word-finding difficulty, the child needs to learn strategies to help him retrieve the word (see advice on word finding in pp.74–75). If you suspect he does not know enough words to express his meaning, his understanding needs checking. Deliberate teaching of specific words to replace empty words should follow (see advice on vocabulary development in RV) (pp.4–24). If you feel the child understands more words than he uses, you need to encourage him to use the vocabulary he knows. Some children are reluctant to speak out in case they are wrong, particularly if there has been, or is, an intelligibility problem. Other children are reserved by nature. In all cases, the child needs to feel it is safe to speak out and that his contribution is welcomed. He will feel safer in a supportive one-to-one setting to start with, then in a small group with familiar children before expecting him to speak out in class.

A child is more likely to learn and use a word if there is a need for him to use it and it is relevant to him. This need can be very motivating and gives language a function. It works best when the equipment and activities are suitable for his developmental age and are interesting.

Techniques to encourage more specific use of vocabulary

Children often use **get** or **put** for specific verbs. Notice and keep a record of the specific words the child is avoiding, and try to encourage him to use them, using the following techniques.

Forced alternatives

Ask the child questions such as, 'Is the boy **sleeping** or **jumping**?', 'Is it a **cat** or a **mouse**?'

Verbal absurdities

Point to a cow and say, 'This is a pig.' (Make sure the child knows this is a game!) His response should be to produce the correct word, 'No, it's not, it's a cow!' Other types of absurdities might be, 'John is drinking his dinner', and questions like, 'Do cats bark?' Alternatively, read a familiar story or rhyme substituting some words and encouraging the child to correct you.

Instructing others

Encourage the child to tell another what to do, such as, **take, hold, keep, grab, bounce, throw** the ball. You will need to tell him the word, and then ask him to think of other things that can be done to a ball.

Action pictures

Use pictures of people doing things and encourage the child to copy by telling him what to do. (The second child does not see the picture!)

Barrier games

Put a barrier between two children so each cannot see what the other is doing. Use a matrix of nine numbered squares. Each child has an identical set of nine pictures – animals, activities, etc. Each child has to tell the other to put a certain picture into a numbered square (as in lotto/bingo) by describing, not naming, the picture.

EV3 Expressive vocabulary: IEP targets

These should be **S**pecific, **M**easurable, **A**chievable, **R**elevant, **T**imed (i.e. **SMART**).
   Choose the most appropriate from the list below:

- **learn and use topic vocabulary** (*specify*)
- **reduce use of 'empty' words**
    - by extending use of vocabulary – *see EV2* (pp.76–77)
    - describing 'lost' words by category/function – *see EV1* (pp.74–75)
    - responding to phonological/semantic cueing – *see EV1* (pp.74–75)

(*specify*)
with support/independently.

EG1 Development of sentence grammar

Most children develop sentence grammar in a predictable way, although some children have particular difficulty with certain forms, for example with auxiliary verbs.

The Sentence grammar checklist (p.80) shows how sentence grammar develops. Children tend to use Level I grammar before Level II, and so on. It is no use trying to encourage the child to use the conjunctions **but** or **because** if he is only using **and** with nouns, whatever age he is. In this case he needs encouragement to use **and** with verbs and phrases such as 'running **and** jumping' and 'the red coat **and** the blue ball' before encouraging the use of **but** and **because** at the beginning of sentences, and to link clauses.

Similarly, a child is not likely to have use of a range of auxiliary verbs such as **are**, **were** or **can** if he is not using **is**.

It is worth collecting a sample of the child's spoken language, perhaps by looking at a picture, asking questions, and taping or writing down the responses he makes. A suitable picture might be an illustration of the nursery rhyme, 'This Little Pig'. You can ask questions such as, 'Who has the dinner?', 'What is this pig going to do?', 'What has happened to this pig?', 'What is this pig doing?', 'Tell me all about what is happening.' You may also need samples of things the child says to you or another child.

Date the sentence grammar checklist and, using the key, mark your findings. See if there are any conspicuous gaps. For example, a child who otherwise uses Level IV syntax may still be using very immature pronouns, saying things such as, '**Me** go and get it.'

When you have the information based on your observations, model and encourage the child, using the games suggested, to use the next most mature grammatical feature. Aim to fill any gaps in particular areas and then move the child on, level by level. Update periodically.

Ideas to teach specific difficulties are found in the rest of the EG materials, pp.81–89.

EG2 Sentence grammar checklist

	LEVEL I	LEVEL II	LEVEL III	LEVEL IV	LEVEL V	LEVEL VI
Articles and prepositions	a	the	an at for	from of with		
Pronouns	I me you it	he she him her	we they us them	myself	yourself himself herself itself ourselves themselves	who which that where how when *within sentences*
Possessive	my your mine yours	his her hers	our ours their theirs	*possessive* -s *possessive* its		
Demonstratives and quantifiers	this that	here there	these those something somebody someone	nothing nobody no-one	everything everybody everyone	anything anybody anyone
Plurals	*endings in* -s	*endings in* -es		*endings in* -ves	men women children teeth feet mice	sheep deer
Conjunctions	and *with nouns*	and *with verbs and phrases*	but because *starting sentences*	so but because *within sentences*	or if *within sentences*	if *starting sentences*
Positive verbs	is *with nouns and adjectives*	is + ing *with verbs*	present tense *ending in* -s am/are was/were can	am/are/is going to *past tense ending in* -ed *irregular past tenses*	*more irregular past tenses* will have/has have (got) to must	do does did would could should might *irregular past participles*
Negative verbs		is not/isn't *with nouns and adjectives*	is not + ing can't don't	am/are not was/were not does not won't	did not	have/has not must not
Verb questions		Is? *with nouns and adjectives*	Is + ing?	Isn't? Am/are? Was/were? Can? Do? Does?	Did? Will?	Have? Has?
Interrogatives	What? *with nouns*	Who? Where? What? *with verbs* What for?	When? How? How many? How much?	Why?	Whose? Which?	

Key
x = doesn't know
u = understands
√ = uses

Child's name:

School:

D.o.B.:

Update [   ]   Update [   ]   Update [   ]

EG3 Determiners

Determiners are the words **a**, **the**, **an** and are used with nouns. Some children are slow to develop consistent and appropriate use of determiners.

Games that involve modelling and repetition of the target phrases:

- **Touch and say**. Collect a small selection of toys or pictures. Take turns to say, 'Here is **a** . . .', or 'This is **a** . . .', or 'I like **the** . . .'
- **Give me**. Have a small selection of toys or pictures and take turns to say, 'Give me **the** . . .', or 'Give me **a** . . .'
- **Guess what?** Start drawing simple objects. The child must try to guess what it is, 'It is **a** . . .', or 'Is it **a** . . .?'
- **Pass it on**. In a group, the children must instruct each other to pass on objects, pictures, etc. using the words, 'Give **the** . . . to . . .'

At a later stage, any of these games can be used with names of things that start with vowel sounds so that **an** can be modelled and practised.

EG4 Teaching the copula

The copula is the verb 'to be' used in isolation. It has the forms: **am, are, is, was, were**. 'Am', 'is' and 'are' can be used to join descriptive words to their subjects, e.g.

The book **is** blue.
The houses **are** big.
She **is** pretty.
I **am** big.

This is best taught when teaching vocabulary of size, shape, colour and other attributes.

Ideas for games

- **Big and little**. Have a selection of toys or other objects both large and small. Sort according to size, and say, 'This **is** a big bear. What **is** yours?' encouraging and modelling correct responses.
- **Animal colours**. Use a selection of animal cards and a selection of colour cards. Turn over one of the animal cards and then a colour card and say, 'The cow **is** . . .' and encourage the child to supply the correct answer. After modelling, the child can then take turns.
- **Opposites**. Find some pictures depicting opposites, e.g. big/small boy, dirty/clean shoe, happy/sad clown, and so on. Describe each picture, then place them all face down in matching pairs. Take turns selecting a picture but do not show one another. The other player then guesses, '**Is** the clown happy?' Reply, 'No he**'s** not/Yes he **is**.' Take turns.

These activities can be varied to elicit the past tense **was** and **were**.

EG5 Auxiliary verbs

- Every sentence needs a verb, which is a word which describes an action or state. Sometimes verbs stand on their own, e.g. '**kick**'. They may have a subject, as in '**I** kick', or an object, as in 'kick **the ball**'.
- The endings of verbs change to show when the action happens, for example, if it is in the past, as in, 'he kick**ed**'.
- The ending of a verb can also show how many people or things are being talked about. For example, if **he/she/it** is the subject, then the verb always ends in '**s**' in the present tense, as in '**he** kick**s**', '**she** laugh**s**', '**it** fall**s**'.
- Auxiliary verbs are used with main verbs to change the meaning. For instance, 'he kicked' is about an action that took place at a particular time. 'He was kicking', suggests that the action is temporary.
- Auxiliary verbs are also used to show the time of an action. They can show whether the action is in the past, 'I **went** home', the present, 'He **is** eating', or the future, 'I **will** go to bed.'

The main auxiliary verbs are: do, does, did; have, has, had; am, are, is, was, were.

Other auxiliary verbs include: can, could; may, might; shall, should; will, would; used to; must; ought to.

Auxiliary verbs are used in making:

- Negative statements, as in: 'I **am not** sleeping', 'You **can not** sit here', 'He **was not** eating.' In these cases, the negative word **not** is placed after the auxiliary verb and before the main verb.
- Passive statements. This is when the action is stressed more than the person doing the action, or when the person responsible for the action is not known, as in:
    The window **has been** broken by Gary.
    The food **has been** eaten.
- Question forms. To ask a question, the auxiliary verb is usually put in front of the main verb, as in:
    You **have** eaten my apple. (statement)
    Have you eaten my apple? (question)

In some questions, '**do**' is used instead of the auxiliary verb, as in: '**Do** you want an apple?'

Teaching auxiliary verbs

Here are some games that can be played with a child or children. They require a clear model.

- **Do and say**. An action is performed and the child has to describe the action by following the pattern, 'He **is** sitting', 'I **am** jumping', etc. Take turns.
- **Touch and say**. Use pictures, touch and say words such as, 'She **is** sleeping', 'He **is** reading', etc.
- **Matrix game**. Make a matrix of six or nine squares. Draw in differently coloured shapes. Take turns to say things such as, 'Find a circle that **is** red', 'Find a triangle that **isn't** blue.'

- **Grid game**. Make a grid of toys, animals, mini beasts etc. (The squares can be numbered.) One child asks others to identify the objects/creature using the pattern, 'Which one **is** big but **isn't** a dog', 'Tell me the one which **has** . . . but **hasn't** . . .'
- **Copy me**. Perform an action and ask the child to answer the questions, 'What **were** you doing?', 'What **was** I doing?'
- **Simon did**. Ask the child to copy an action, as in 'Simon Says', and respond to 'What **was** Simon doing?' etc.
- **Yes/no game**. This is useful for the whole class, for two or three minutes at the end of a lesson, as well as in individual work. The children don't know they are required to supply an auxiliary verb in order to respond. They are told they must not answer yes/no or they are out. Ask questions such as, '**Do** you **have** a brother?' This forces the child to respond using the auxiliary verb '**have**', as in 'I **have**'/'I **haven't**'. Other types of question would be '**Did** your mum bring you to school?', '**Are** you six?', '**Is** the book blue?' You can give a clue to the child by saying that the word to help him is in the question.

It is often easier to teach auxiliary verbs in negatives and questions first, before expecting their use in statements. Use the full form first, e.g. **is not**, rather than the contracted form **isn't**.

EG6 Negatives

Children usually start to use negation by saying things such as, '**No** do this', 'That **not** a dog', and 'I **not** touch.' When they can use auxiliary verbs they develop the correct forms as in, 'I **can't** do this', 'That's **not** a dog', and 'I'm **not** touching.'

The child must learn to put the **not** (or **n't**) after the first auxiliary verb. A child will not use correct negatives until he is using the auxiliaries correctly. It is often useful to teach them both together and then they can be used for contrast.

Useful early auxiliary verbs are: is, can, have, do.
Useful early negatives are: isn't, can't, haven't, don't.

Ideas for teaching negatives

- **Touch and say**. Use people, toys etc., to say, for example, 'He is sitting/he **isn't** sitting', 'You have long hair/I **haven't** got long hair.'
- **Say and do**. Describe actions with words such as, 'I can stand on one leg/You **can't** stand on one leg.'
- **Look and say**. Describe pictures of animals in terms of what they can do, e.g. 'The fish can . . .', 'The dog **can't** . . .'
- **I don't like but . . .** Taking it in turns, ask other children what they do and don't like. Offer a model to encourage response such as, 'I **don't** like onions but I do like chocolate.'
- **Child has/hasn't**. Use figures of children with different attributes and dressed differently. Take turns to describe the pictures with the target words, for example, 'She has trousers but she **hasn't** . . .'
- **Nonsense questions**. Use pictures or objects and ask silly questions such as, 'Is it a pencil?' when pointing to something else. The target response, which may want modelling, would be, 'No it **isn't**, it's a (chair).'

EG7 Question forms

Children first ask questions by saying single words with a rising intonation, which will require a yes/no answer, for example, 'car?' meaning 'Are we going in the car?' They then go on to develop the 'wh' question words, which are put at the beginning of a sentence. At about 18 months to two years, their questions will take the form, '**What** that?', '**What** he do?'

At about two to two and a half years, their questions will sound like, '**What** man doing?', '**Where** horse go?', '**What** getting?', '**Why** you cross?' By three years old, they will be using the auxiliary verb but not inverting it, as in; '**Why I can't** have it?', '**Where** the book **is**?'

From about the age of three years onwards, the auxiliary verb is usually properly inverted, as in, '**Where is** the glass of milk?' They then start to use the auxiliaries at the beginning of sentences, as in, '**Are** you going?', '**Can** I do that?', '**Will** you give it to me?', '**Do** you want a biscuit?'

Some ideas for teaching these words are included in section RV9 (pp.16–17). Here are some more ideas:

- **OXO game**. Write target question words on separate pieces of card. Take it in turns to turn them over. Ask an appropriate question beginning with the word turned up. The next step is to place the words in a noughts and crosses grid (OXO) and try to be the first to get three in a row.
- **What am I?** Think of a place, person or object. Take turns to describe and then guess, e.g. 'I have four legs and I am made of wood. What am I?'
- **Questionnaires**. Ask questions to gain information for graphs, charts etc. In order to collect the information the children must be able to ask questions such as, '**How** did you come to school?', '**What** did you have for breakfast?', '**Which** is your favourite TV programme?'
- **What's in the bag?** Toys, familiar objects etc. are put into a bag. One child knows what the object is while the others have to try to work it out, asking questions such as, '**Where** is it from?', '**What** is it for?', '**What** is it made out of?', '**Who** uses it?'
- **Group news**. The children listen to each other's news and ask each other specific questions. For instance, a child might say, 'I stayed at my Nana's.' This could be followed up with, '**How** long did you stay?', '**What** did you do?', '**Where** did you sleep?'

Another way of asking a question is to put the auxiliary verb in front of the subject of the sentence. When this happens, the 'wh' question words are not used.

Some ideas to teach verb inversion in questions

- **Eyes closed**. Encourage the child to act while you close your eyes. Ask, '**Are you** jumping/sitting?' The child should reply, 'I am/I'm not.' Reverse roles, encouraging 'are' first.
- **Ask a silly question**. Use 'can' as the first word. Take turns to ask silly question, such as, '**Can** pigs fly?', '**Can** balls eat?'
- **Shopkeeper**. The child is the shopkeeper with various objects to sell. You pretend you can't remember what you want, so the child has to say, '**Do you** want sweets?', '**Do you** want a teddy?' etc. Vary this so the child has to ask, using the form you model, such as, '**Can I** have a teddy?', '**May** I have an apple?' etc.

EG8 Using the past tenses of verbs

Difficulties using the past tense of verbs usually arise in one or more areas:

- marking the past tense with **-ed** endings (skipp**ed**, cook**ed** etc.)
- describing the past using an auxiliary verb (**was** crying, **were** running etc.)
- using irregular verbs (as in 'he mak**ed**' instead of 'he made').

Children usually learn to use past tenses in this order, and specific teaching should follow the same developmental pattern.

Ideas for teaching '-ed' endings

- **Copy me**. Perform an action and ask the child to answer the question, 'What did I do?'
- **Simon did**. Ask the child to copy an action as in 'Simon Says', and then ask, 'What happened?'
- **Lift the flaps**. Action pictures can be covered with paper and numbered. Roll a dice and ask the child to lift the flap and answer the question, 'What happened?'
- **Walkabout**. Take the child (or toy animals) to different places around the school or classroom, and help him to say, 'We walk**ed** . . .' or ' He walk**ed** . . .'

Irregular verbs are best taught through modelling and correcting as and when an incorrect form emerges in the child's language. Older children who are having difficulties may need more specific teaching with regular testing until learning is established.

Teaching ideas for irregular past tense endings

- **Walkabout**. Take the child (or toy) to different places in the school or room, and help him to say, 'We **went** to . . .', 'He **went** to . . .'
- **Actions/action pictures**. Encourage the child to respond appropriately to questions requiring an irregular past tense verb, such as:
    'What did he make/throw/take/see/draw?' etc.
    'Where did he buy/ride/run/fall/stand?' etc.

EG9 Joining words

Children first start using '**and**' to join nouns, as in 'fish and chips'; verbs, as in 'running and jumping' and to connect simple sentences and ideas. However they need to develop more ways of connecting ideas. These words tend to be learned after 'and': so, so that, if, or, because, but. They express different and more complex relationships between ideas.

Some children do not learn to use these words – other children use them in the wrong place, therefore they need to be taught. The following ideas will help the child to join sentences:

- **Story sequence**. Take turns to describe something the child has done, or describe a sequence of pictures with the words '**and then**' between each turn. Well-known stories such as 'The Three Bears' can be a starting point.
- **Do one more**. Take turns to perform a simple action such as jumping. Another child copies the first action and adds one more, saying, 'I can jump **and** hop as well.' This can be extended to include several actions.
- **And so**. Use objects with similar characteristics. Say, 'The car is red **and so** is the bus.' Encourage child to use 'and so' after modelling.
- **Picture pairs**. Take pairs of pictures illustrating purpose, e.g. a child taking off his clothes, a child in bath; a child opening a jar, a child taking out a biscuit, etc. The target utterance is 'The girl opens the jar **so** she can have a biscuit' etc.
- **If picture pairs**. Collect picture pairs illustrating a consequence, e.g. a child dropping a cup, a broken cup; a child watering a plant, a large flowering plant. The target utterance is, '**If** you drop a cup, it will break' etc.
- **Pretend**. Ask questions such as, 'If you were a queen, what would you wear?', varying the person. A variation would be something like, '**If** I had three wishes **then** . . .'
- **Forced alternatives**. Use toys and tokens. Offer a choice between two articles, saying, 'You can have the red car or you can have the blue car', etc. Encourage the child to use '**or**' and ask others to choose between two things.
- **Why/because?** Use LDA pictures (available from Learning Development Aids, Cambridge, or similar) to ask why something is happening, e.g. ambulance hurrying to an accident, or a muddy boy holding a football. Model and encourage an appropriate response beginning with '**because**'.
- **Odd one out**. Either use pictures or objects and describe the odd one out, e.g. 'These are red/round/big etc. **but** this one isn't.'

EG10 Expressing ideas

Some children have real difficulty expressing their ideas in language. They may have a rather general idea of what they want to say, but have difficulty formulating it. Suspect this if you notice the child has the following difficulties:

- word order problems
- omission of key words or phrases
- lack of sentence variety, e.g. constant use of subject–verb–object sentences
- a tendency to string words together with little sentence structure and often with some jargon words
- a tendency to start a sentence, trail off and try again
- a discrepancy between the child's ability to respond to simple questions about picture material and extreme difficulty in spontaneously communicating information.

It will help the child if he is asked to focus on the verb of his message, whether that is a statement or a question. Use questions such as 'what's **happening**?', 'what is he **doing**?', 'what do you want me to **do**?'

When he has chosen his verb, for example 'shopping', you can then ask '**who** is doing it?' Follow this with a '**what**' question if appropriate. For instance, if he had chosen 'throw' as his verb, and 'Tom' as the actor/subject, he would need an object such as 'the snowball'. 'Shopping' could be followed by a question such as '**what for**?'

At this stage see if the child can give you the sentence so far, such as:

Mum went shopping for trainers.
Tom threw the snowball.
Dad cooked dinner.

Next ask '**where** is it happening?'
'in Newcastle'
'in the playground'
'at my house'

Ask '**who gets** it?', '**who** does he **do it to**?'
'for my brother'
'at David'
'for me'

To elicit a description ask other questions, depending on the verb, such as '**what like**?', '**what** colour?', '**how**?', '**how** did he throw it?' Always ask for the verb and the actor/subject, and ask other questions as appropriate. Say things such as, 'You haven't told me **who** did it', and '**What** do you want me to **do**?'

Encourage the child to express what he wants in one or two sentences. Use this procedure systematically so that he can develop it as a strategy to help him order his thoughts and formulate his sentences.

EG11 Expressive grammar: IEP targets

These should be **S**pecific, **M**easurable, **A**chievable, **R**elevant, **T**imed (i.e. **SMART**). Choose the most appropriate from the list below:

- **use determiners a/the/an** – *see EG3* (p.81)
- **use am/are/is/was/were** – *see EG4* (p.82)
- **use the auxiliary verbs is, was, were/am, are/do, does, did/have, has, had/can, could/may, might/shall, should/will, would/used to/must/ought to** – *specify* – *see EG5* (pp.83–84)
- **use auxiliary verbs in negative statements/questions** – *see EG5 and EG6* (pp.83–86)
- **use 'wh' question forms with inversion** – *see EG7* (p.86) *and RV9* (pp.16–17)
- **use auxiliary verbs at the beginning of questions** – *see EG7* (p.86)
- **use '-ed' endings in past tense verbs** – *see EG8* (p.87)
- **learn and use correct past tense auxiliary verbs** – *see EG8* (p.87)
- **expand use of joining words to include so/so that/if /or/because/but** – *specify* – *see EG9* (p.89)

(*specify*)
in short sentences/in structured situations/in spontaneous speech/with/without adult prompts.

SPOKEN LANGUAGE

S1 Spoken language difficulties in the classroom

General classroom strategies

- Children may use language spontaneously in certain situations while avoiding others. Observe and note down when and with whom they seem happiest to talk. Gradually try to extend these times.
    - The teacher, another adult or a couple of chosen pupils could join the child in his 'comfortable' activity.
    - Arrange for familiar children and adults, with whom the child talks spontaneously, to join the child at other times, when he has been less willing to talk.
- Encourage the child to use other non-verbal means of conveying information alongside his speech. He could use gesture, objects or drawings to help get his message across.
- Do allow other children to interpret for the child if he will accept this.
- Do not pressure the child to change his speech or speak in front of a group if he is obviously unwilling to do so. In situations when everyone is expected to give a verbal reply, such as registration, you could agree a form of verbal reply with the child so that he is seen to be like everyone else, but is not put under pressure to attempt what is, for him, an unpronounceable teacher's name.
- Encourage the use of language in a variety of situations and for a variety of purposes – social, in play, making requests, giving responses. The teacher may need to give models of language and suggest what the child may say. However, do not pressure the child to talk in unfamiliar situations until he is comfortable in situations of his own choice.
- Create opportunities to involve the child in paired and small-group activities with classmates. The child may need to be given a definite role in the group, so games involving turn-taking are useful. Group or paired activities can help to encourage listening skills, turn-taking and cooperative play which the child may find difficult within the larger group.
- Choose reading books that have simple sentences, as near to 'natural' sentence structures as possible.
- Allow the child to produce written sentences at his own level, using a 'breakthrough' approach.
- A child who has a speech difficulty may need much deliberate teaching of listening and auditory skills, such as rhyme, initial sounds, segmentation and memory.

S2 Listening and communicating with an unintelligible child

When a child in your class has difficulty making himself understood because of unintelligible speech and/or disordered expressive language:

- Let the child know that you want to understand him and help him get his message across. Arrange to talk with the child when you are least likely to be interrupted – a few minutes to talk or hear reading at the beginning of break/lunch time may be possible, or any time when other children will not be competing for your attention.
- Do, if necessary, admit that you have not quite understood everything that the child has said. Acknowledge the part(s) that you *have* understood and ask the child to tell, or demonstrate the other bit again. Always accept that *you* have a problem in understanding – it is the child's job to help you understand.
- Repeat the child's sentence 'correctly' to confirm that you have understood and to give a simple model, for imitation. The child may imitate an adult model but do not pressure him to do so.
- Talk about events that are 'here and now':
  - to help the child's understanding if he has comprehension problems;
  - to focus the child's direction if he has attention problems;
  - as a point of reference for the child and teacher in the presence of expressive language problems.
- Children are likely to talk most successfully about familiar events. A home/school book can be helpful and the child could be encouraged to bring objects/photographs from home.
- Provide a framework to guide the child's talk. A sequence of pictures or key objects can guide the recounting of an event or story.

S3 Children who stammer

- Try to arrange some time in the day when you can give him some undivided attention without being interrupted.
- Try to get on the same level as the child when you want him to speak to you so he does not feel intimidated.
- Listen carefully, concentrating on the content of what he is saying, not how he is saying it.
- Don't look away from the child when he is stammering. Don't finish off what he is trying to say unless you are sure he wants you to. Give him time to finish, or try a new way of getting his message across.
- Slow down your own rate of talking so that the child does not try to match the rate of his speech with yours.
- Reduce the number of questions you ask. Give him time to answer one before going on to another. If he is struggling, and you are fairly sure of what he is likely to say, you could say things like 'Did you see it here or in the cloakroom?' He will benefit from an alternative being modelled.
- Be aware of the times when he is having most difficulty so that they can be avoided. Likely times are when he is being interrupted or hurried; when he is competing to speak; fear of the consequences of what he is saying; expressing complex ideas; using relatively new vocabulary and sentence structures.
- If registration is a problem, together with the child try to find alternative ways of responding, perhaps with a form of words he can say fluently.
- Encourage awareness of turn-taking for all the children in the class. Don't allow others to interrupt him or for him to interrupt others.
- Stammering children can have very low self-esteem, so praise the child when he does anything good. Let him know you value the contribution he does make in other ways.
- Don't allow him to do things you would not allow other children to do just because he has difficulties. Discipline should be just as appropriate and consistent for him as for others.
- The child is likely to do best when he is calm. He is not likely to flourish in an environment of unexpected change.

S4 Inappropriate speech styles

- Some children speak too loudly with a lack of variation in pitch, stress and rhythm in a monotonous tone. Some have over-precise diction and stress every syllable. Quite often children on the autistic spectrum speak inappropriately – their speech is sometimes described as 'adultified' and can sound pompous in a child.
- There may be little understanding of what other people are thinking or feeling, and that how the child speaks may embarrass people they are with.
- Difficulty 'reading' non-verbal expressions and body language means that embarrassment in other people may not be recognised.
- Inappropriate volume may indicate anxiety.

Ideas to try

- Check that the child's hearing is within normal range.
- Model normal volume for speaking and encourage the child to practise in different situations.
- Use a non-verbal cue, such as a finger over the lips, when the child is speaking too loudly.
- Record the child talking in different situations and evaluate the appropriateness of his volume together. Tell him that others have difficulties understanding him when he talks too loudly. Explain what those difficulties are – he may not realise it for himself.
- If the tone of voice is monotonous, seek advice from a drama teacher or speech and language therapist.
- Play games that require him to whisper, such as 'Chinese Whispers'.

S5 The young non-speaking child

Strategies

Some children refuse to speak in some situations. They often speak freely at home and sometimes outside, but they won't speak to family members outside the home. Usually this selective speaking only becomes a problem when they enter nursery or school. The act of speaking has become associated with severe anxiety in certain situations and the child copes with this problem by staying silent. Parents of children who won't speak often describe them as 'shy and stubborn'.

Confrontation only makes the situation worse. When first admitted to school or playgroup the following strategies may help to reduce the child's anxiety and, in less severe cases, may be sufficient to enable the child to speak freely in the new setting:

- Present a reassuring, approving and smiling face. Let the child know that you enjoy being with him ('This is fun!') – that you like him for himself rather than for his speech.
- Treat the child in just the same way as the others – do not make special concessions for him or let him think you regard him as 'the child who does not speak'. Once established, this role is difficult to climb down from.
- Try not to be hurt or offended when he does not talk to you – remember that the child feels worse than you do.
- Never beg, bribe or challenge the child to speak, or let on how important it is to you to hear him talk.
- Once it is obvious that the child is going to remain silent on this occasion, treat this very calmly and unemotionally, moving on swiftly before panic has time to set in, e.g. 'Well, I don't blame you for not wanting to go – I'm not keen on climbing frames either', 'That's OK, it doesn't matter if you're not sure – let's see if Mark knows the answer.' Give the child the impression that you regard his silence as a lack of desire or knowledge rather than an inability to speak. Not only does this remove a lot of the pressure (and therefore anxiety), it provides far greater motivation to speak than the satisfaction of speech for its own sake.
- Avoid asking direct questions that put the child in a 'no-win' situation. He will feel anxious both about answering and not answering. Instead, provide opportunities for him to comment if he feels sufficiently comfortable, e.g. 'I love this colour – I wonder what your favourite colour is?', 'Look at this! I bet you haven't seen one of those before', 'I wonder . . .', 'I bet . . .', 'I (don't) suppose . . .', 'I guess . . .', are extremely useful phrases as they invite a response, rather than demand it.
- Avoid looking directly at the child after providing the opportunity to speak.
- Turn your ear towards the child so that an answer can be whispered if the child prefers.
- Provide opportunities to speak without putting the child directly 'under the spotlight'. Avoid situations where other children or adults are watching and waiting for the child to speak.
- Try to find time to be alone with the child on his own at your desk or in a quiet room, again providing opportunities rather than imperatives to talk. However, this must never become a special privilege for not talking – it should be apparent that other children have a turn too.

- Give the child jobs to do that provide opportunities for speech in situations which he finds less threatening, e.g. 'Can you take (new child) to the pegs and show her where to put her PE bag?', 'Take Mummy to the hall and show her the models we've been making for assembly', 'Please help (less able child) tidy up – he's not sure what he's got to do.'

- For the child in more formal education it is possible to deliver much of the curriculum (rather than general conversation and participation) through non-verbal means. This would include drawing, picture/word selection, picture/word matching, puzzle completion and writing. This can be done very matter-of-factly in the same way as you would differentiate the curriculum for any child. If restricted to classwork or more formal table-top activities, these non-verbal methods need not be regarded as an acceptable alternative to speech.

- Concentrate on providing an enjoyable, relaxing environment where you gain the child's trust through demonstrations of approval. If there is no change after a few weeks and if you feel confident that you have established the necessary rapport, acknowledge the problem with the child. Make these points to him:
  - you know it's hard for him to talk
  - other children feel just like he does
  - one day it won't be so bad and he'll feel good enough to speak
  - you can wait until that time comes
  - it wouldn't be fair to the others if he was treated differently
  - so he must just join in as much as possible.

S6 The older non-speaking child

The school can attempt to aid progress by:

- Keeping a written record of occasions when the child communicates with staff and peers in lessons.
- Ensuring that all staff are aware that the record sheets are to be completed.
- Rewarding through the merit system when there is verbal communication.
- Discouraging other pupils to 'speak for' the child. Encourage the child's independence. Talk with other pupils about the need for the child to be independent.
- Providing opportunities for the child to sit with/work with pupils outside the child's usual social group. Paired reading with a younger child may be useful. Slowly work towards working in a slightly larger group so there is a need to communicate with more children.
- Ensuring the class teacher is sympathetic to the child's needs, possibly acting as a mentor. The school needs to think about the age/position of the mentor, how and when it can work, and which situations need it the most.
- Involving the child in choosing target setting for the IEP. He could be involved in drawing up targets, perhaps in the form of a tick list that could be completed regularly (daily/weekly). The list could include targets such as answering the register, asking one question a day of a specific teacher, responding with a 'yes' or a 'no' to a request from any other child outside of his immediate circle (this can be set up!). These targets can be modified to reflect the child's needs at any one time.
- Recognising that the child wants success while not wanting to be noticed. A system of Records of Achievement could be instituted taking into account not only academic progress but any progress with social and communication skills. The child needs to know that other people, outside of the immediate circle, will value his spoken communication and that the school wants to help.
- Establishing an expectation that the child will contribute at the same level as other pupils, even if the means used is another form of communication, such as agreed non-verbal signals and in writing.
- Encouraging the child to verbalise wishes, even if this necessitates using a small number of words such as 'please help' when help is required from the teacher.
- Reviewing the child's objectives half-termly.
- Encouraging the use of drama, particularly in small groups.
- Asking the child to sing, say a rhyme etc. at home and bring the recording to school so that other pupils can hear the child's natural voice. Taping could also be done at lunch times.
- Encouraging the older child to take part in choirs, music club, drama clubs etc.
- Providing opportunities, as appropriate, for the child with the teacher/mentor to reflect on difficulties with talking and communication, and feelings about school. Explore as appropriate particular areas of difficulty, e.g. mixing with other pupils, making friends and tensions which arise in interpersonal situations. When the child is anxious, these feelings might be accompanied by changes in physical states. The child could be helped to be aware of these changes and may be willing to write about them. This information could be used to help develop strategies to monitor and avoid stress, for example by deep breathing. Other strategies to help avoid and defuse anxiety may be helpful.

- Understanding the difficulty the child may have with transitions, particularly between year groups and especially between phase changes. It may be helpful for the teacher/mentor from the receiving school to visit the child at home. Teachers from the receiving school need to know of the child's difficulties in advance and should not challenge the child with direct questions. They should find alternative ways to assess his understanding in class.

Parents can help by:

- providing opportunities to talk on the phone to family
- encouraging the child to phone friends
- inviting friends around for tea to socialise
- encouraging taping of the child singing and talking
- encouraging joining after-school clubs.

S7 Speech: IEP targets

These should be **S**pecific, **M**easurable, **A**chievable, **R**elevant, **T**imed (i.e. **SMART**). Choose the most appropriate from the list below:

- **be willing to speak in a wider range of settings – in a small group/in class/in the dinner hall/in the playground/to other children/to other adults** *– specify – see S1* (p.91), *S3 (p.93), S5 and S6 (pp.95–98)*
- **correctly repeat adult-modelled words/sentences** *– see S2 (p.92)*
- **speak with normal volume with/without adult prompts** *– see S4 (p.94)*
- **slow down the rate of delivery** *– see S4 (p.94)*.

PLAY SKILLS

P1 Language and play

Language development is stimulated through play. Through play, children develop new skills and practise skills they already have. They learn to listen, share, observe and imitate.

Play develops through different stages.

- It starts with **exploratory play**. The child sucks, bangs and drops things.
- This progresses to **functional play**, when the child uses toys without any pretence, such as putting a cup on a saucer or putting one brick on top of another.
- **Pretend play** follows. At the early stages the child may pretend to feed himself. This develops into object substitution, for example when the child pretends the wooden block is a car. This is a vital stage, and shows that the child has learned that one object can substitute for another. One object can now be a symbol for something else.
- The next step is when the child attributes **false properties** to an object in play, such as washing the doll's face as if it was dirty, or pretending to comfort a crying baby. The child has now learned that things stay as they really are, even when people pretend they are something else.
- The final stage is when the child uses **imaginary objects** in play, for example drinking from an empty cup. The child has learned that it is possible to pretend that there is something there when in reality there isn't.

The ability to use **symbolic play** (i.e. object substitution, attributing false properties to objects and using imaginary objects in play) means that through pretence, the child has many more opportunities to use vocabulary and develop increasingly mature spoken language. Sequences of pretend play help the child to link ideas.

When working with a young child on any aspect of language development, it is important to relate what is done to the **developmental play** level of the child. He has to first learn to play with objects before using them to represent other objects. He must do this before he can understand that pictures, too, represent objects, situations and states of mind.

The final step is when the child understands that sounds can be represented by symbols called letters and that objects, situations and states can be represented by sequences of symbols called words and sentences.

P2 Communication and play

Children progress from vocalised dialogues to conversational turn-taking, parallel play then cooperative play.

Babies have to communicate their feelings, desires and intentions through non-verbal means such as crying, pointing, waving and laughing. This develops into dialogues if the adult responds as if the baby had really verbalised communication. (You want the teddy, do you?) The dialogues involve vocalising, making movements and pausing, and naturally teaches turn-taking, as in:

Adult: Say bye bye Gran. (adult waves baby's hand) You say it. (pause) Bye bye Gran. (wave, pause)
Baby: ba-ba. (waves hand)
Adult: That's right, bye bye Gran. (wave, pause)
Baby: ba-ba. (waves)

Words and phrases start to slot into the 'conversation' which is now ready for words.

Most children play alongside others, in **parallel play**, before they start to develop **cooperative play**, which is reciprocal and involves sharing interests, looking, listening and taking turns. When the child reaches this stage, he is able to learn much more in all kinds of ways from the people around him.

Babies learn from imitating adults, however some children do not naturally do this. Other children have difficulty with social timing, preventing effective dialogue. While most children are instinctively interested in things that others are doing, some children have difficulty understanding shared attention, for instance not looking at what is being pointed to or being able to share a book.

In order to help these children learn to take turns, use eye contact and enjoy shared experiences – the adult needs to join the child in his social world. It is important that efforts to extend the child's play and communication skills are pitched at the appropriate level, i.e. **where he is now**, and then extended to the next level. Do not expect cooperative play of a child who is uninterested in others and has difficulty with social timing.

P3 Play skills: IEP targets

These should be Specific, Measurable, Achievable, Relevant, Timed (i.e. **SMART**). Choose the most appropriate from the list below:

- develop pretend play
- attribute false properties to an object in play
- use imaginary objects in play
- develop pretend play into sequences
- understand that pictures represent objects
- understand that letters represent sounds
- understand that words represent objects, situations and states
- develop turn-taking through vocalised dialogues
- watch and imitate others
- develop the ability to share the focus of attention
- play in parallel with one/two/three/four others (*specify*) child/children for (*specify*) minutes
- play cooperatively with one/two/three/four others (*specify*) child/children for (*specify*) minutes.

USE OF LANGUAGE

UL1 Conveying information

Some children tend to give the minimum information and rely on others to ask more questions if more information is needed. Sometimes they are just not aware of what a listener needs to know, or how much information a listener already has.

In these cases, do not speak for the child or supply his answers. Encourage him to tell you more, saying that you do not know, for example, which animal he is talking about, or where it is, or who was carrying the bag, etc. Activities to help teach question words can be useful for this.

Other activities to encourage children to give more information include:

- **Barrier games**. With a barrier between two children, one child instructs another to find a particular picture by describing it.
- **Do as I say**. Decide what you want another child to do. The child has to give all the information to another, for example, 'put the black hat on', 'get the ball', 'touch the wall'. Adapt this to directing the drawing of a picture.
- **Sequences**. Encourage talk about growth sequences such as planting a seed, frogspawn, etc. The child then, perhaps with the aid of three or four pictures, has to explain the sequence to another child.
- **Messenger**. Send the child to another adult (or child) with a message (with at least three parts). Bring back the response.
- **Blindfold**. You put a scarf over your eyes. The child has to describe a picture or toy to you so you can guess what it is. Reverse roles. Try to encourage awareness of the need for information.
- **What am I?** The child has to look at a picture of an object and give two or three clues so another child can guess what it is, such as 'I have four legs. You sit on me.' This can be varied by choosing a person/animal from a familiar story, and saying, for example, 'I went to my grandmother's house. A wolf followed me. I wore a red cloak.'

UL2 Use of language

Children need to use their language for an increasing range of purposes as they grow older.

- When they are young they need to be able to express their needs, feelings and wants. Later they will be able to put their feelings into words.
- They need to use their language to interact with others – to make comments, to volunteer information, to relay messages, to ask for help and clarification. They need to be able to direct others, collaborate with them and accept negotiation.
- When young, they should be able to report on present and past experiences. When they are older they will refer to future events, to sequences of events and make comparisons and connections. They should be able to give a chronological account of an event or story.
- As they learn to reason they will recognise cause and effect, and how events depend on each other. Older children will use their language to predict events, sequences, recognise problems and possible solutions, verbalise alternative courses of actions and predict the consequences of actions and events.
- They will be able to organise activities using their language.
- Children also need to use their language for imaginative purposes, as in role play and in making up stories.

When language is restricted, some children do not naturally develop a full range of language uses, perhaps because of expressive language difficulties, or because, as in children with social interaction difficulties, they do not share the same perceptions so that their language purposes become skewed or circumscribed. Some children lack confidence and do not function well in class settings. Children with certain learning difficulties find it difficult to structure their experience or express their thinking, and their language uses tend to be restricted.

For children to develop a good range of language uses appropriate to their age, they need to be put in situations and have experiences that naturally provoke an extension of use. They need to:

- extend their language uses
- extend the range of settings in which they will use their extended range of language uses.

Ideas to extend use of language

- Refer to the Use of language checklist (p.106) to see if there are any obvious gaps compared to most other children in the class.
- Try to devise activities to help the child start to use or extend his language for a specific purpose.
- Make the activities interesting experiences to motivate the child.
- Use situations that arise naturally, and encourage the child to contribute just a little more.
- The child may need support, particularly at first.
  For instance:
  - speak his response out in class as he whispers it to you
  - go with the child to relay a message, or write it down for him

- use a storyline or mindmap as visual support to the planning of a spoken language activity, e.g. a talk to the class about a pet, the retelling of a story or event, etc.
- use a calendar to talk about past and future events (see pp.20–22).
● Use other children as models to help extend use.
For instance:
  - take turns to speak about last week's news, then next week's news (it can be a fantasy!)
  - play games involving turn-taking and directing others, e.g. 'Tell Tom to put the ball in the bucket and put on the hat.' Circle games can be helpful.
● Be aware of settings, noticing, for example:
  - which other child/children the child is most comfortable with
  - which children are best for modelling activities
  - how many children the child can cope with
  - the best seating position for the child for different activities, in different areas.
● Try to extend the child's range of language uses from one-to-one to small groups, then into whole-class situations.
● Review the child's progress at least termly and adjust targets accordingly.

UL3

Use of language checklist

Name of child: .... **D.o.B.** ....

Class: .... **Teacher:** .... **Year group:** ....

Date: .... **Compiled by:** ....

Does the child:	Spontaneously			With support		
	1:1	Small group	In class	1:1	Small group	In class
respond to questions appropriately?						
volunteer information and make comments?						
state likes/dislikes?						
express feelings in words?						
ask for help/clarification?						
accept negotiation?						
make requests?						
direct others?						
relay messages?						
refer to past/future events?						
role play?						
speculate? (What if . . . ?)						
use language to imagine?						
ask relevant questions at appropriate times?						
organise/plan activities using language?						
give an account of an event or story with some sense of beginning, middle and end?						

UL4 Use of language: IEP targets

These should be Specific, Measurable, Achievable, Relevant, Timed (i.e. **SMART**). Choose the most appropriate from the list below:

- **respond to questions appropriately** – *see UL1* (p.103) *and RV9* (p.16–17)
- **volunteer information to another child/adult/small group/whole class** – *specify* – *see UL1* (p.103)
- **relay a message of two/three parts** – *see UL1* (p.103)
- **talk about the recent past/immediate future** – *see UL2* (pp.104–5)
- **retell a story/recount an event/with a beginning, middle and end** – *see UL2* (pp.104–5)
- **organise own/group activities using language** – *see UL2* (pp.104–5)
- **use language for imaginative purposes/in role play/making up stories** – *see UL2* (pp.104–5)

(*specify*)
with/without adult prompts.

CONVERSATION SKILLS

CS1 Children with immature conversation skills

These children may well also be experiencing receptive and/or expressive language delays because of specific language or general learning difficulties. Like other skills, conversation skills can develop through practice. This practice needs to be:

- appropriate to their age
- appropriate to their language ability.

There are three main areas of difficulty.

Content

- understanding the message
- making comments relevant to the subject being talked about.

Intention

- recognising their own needs and thoughts
- putting these needs and thoughts into words
- making their comments at the right time and in the right place.

Recognising listener needs

- knowing what is shared knowledge
- knowing what details are necessary for the listener to understand the message.

Suggestions to help

Content

- Keep language simple – this will reduce the possibility of the child making an inappropriate response because he hasn't understood.
- Keep on target. Make sure you get the response you want from the child in the end, repeating, rephrasing and modelling as necessary.
- Keep on topic.
    - Don't let the child distract you.
    - Don't let the child go off at a tangent.
    - Keep redirecting the child's focus.
    - Keep questions precise (not open-ended).
    - Narrow the topic down, e.g. talk about a few animals rather than zoos.
- Make boundaries clear.
    - Let the child know that he can answer with one or two words.
    - Stop a talkative child when he has answered the question or conveyed the necessary information.
    - Repeat the essential part of the message.

– You introduce the topic and you end it. Make sure the child knows the conversation has moved on to something else.

Intention

- Ensure there is a *need* to communicate.
    – Don't anticipate the child's needs.
    – Neither you nor other children should talk for him if he is capable of doing it for himself.
    – Create a need for communication, i.e. tell the child to colour something red and give a blue crayon/say 'cut your paper' and give a paintbrush, etc.
- Encourage identifying needs, and being specific.
    – When the child has started a communication but not actually said what he wants, wait, respond neutrally, encouraging further expansion. Prompt with specific questions.
- Don't take the lead.
    – Don't ask too many questions requiring just yes/no answers. Remember, the longer the question the shorter the answer.
    – Make provocative statements such as, 'I've got something exciting in this box', rather than ask closed questions such as, 'Do you want to see what's in this box?'
    – Provide a model to imitate if the child fails to express his intention clearly enough:
        ○ indirectly, as in, 'I'll get the scissors if you want them';
        ○ directly, as in, 'If you want to show me the book, say "Look, Miss Smith".'
    – Try indirect first and be sure the child is capable of copying your model. Don't respond if he doesn't ask correctly after modelling when you know he can.
- Reinforce attempts to express intent.
    – Respond to content.
    – Accept a true attempt, regardless of errors in grammar or pronunciation. This can be corrected later once the child has a basic vocabulary and a desire to express his needs.
    – Reinforce the request by responding immediately and/or praise his utterance with things such as, 'Good asking! You said "apron" so I'll help you with your apron.'
    – Ignore or deflect empty questions. Say, 'Yes, but what we are doing *now* is . . .' and 'I'll answer the question one more time . . . now let's finish the picture', and then ignore it when he repeats the same question.

Recognising listener needs

- Let the child know what has been omitted.
    – Say why you are having difficulty, 'But you haven't said *who* was there', 'You haven't said *where* you were', and 'I don't know where you play because I haven't been there.'
- Help the child to recognise what he doesn't need to say.
    – Say, 'I was there so I know. Tell Tom instead because he wasn't there', 'You've already said "hello" so you don't need to say it again. It will last all day.'

CS2

Conversation skills checklist

Name of child: .... D.o.B. ....

Class: .... Teacher: .... Year group: ....

Date: .... Compiled by: ....

Does the child:	Spontaneously			With support		
	1:1	Small group	In class	1:1	Small group	In class
a) initiate conversation with other children?						
b) take turns to talk?						
c) know when/how to join conversation/stop?						
d) listen to others?						
e) develop conversation beyond one turn?						
f) show awareness of listener's knowledge/ needs?						
g) clarify others' misunderstandings?						
h) supply further information when asked?						
i) know when he/she has misunderstood?						
j) keep to topic?						
k) give relevant and appropriate responses?						
l) understand non-verbal cues (such as facial expressions)?						
m) relate most important points rather than peripheral details?						
n) use an appropriate speech style (not too formal, too loud, too monotonous)?						
o) make appropriate eye contact (looks at the speaker, at the person talked to, length of gaze)?						

CS3 Learning conversational skills

Use the Conversation skills checklist (p.110) to gain a profile of the child's current abilities. The following are some ideas to help children who have difficulty.

Initiating conversation with other children

The child may be shy, the others boisterous, and all may need some help developing appropriate conversation skills.

- Try to engineer situations in which the child has to take the initiative, such as asking questions about other children's news, or sending the child to ask another child a question, preferably one that is not answered with yes or no, such as, 'Miss Smith wants to know when is your birthday.'
- Circle time activities can also be helpful.

Taking turns to talk

Most children have a natural feel for turn-taking, but some children have not had good experiences, or have difficulty with social interaction for a variety of reasons.

- These children need to be taught the '**rules of conversation**':
  - one person talks at a time
  - the others listen
  - they look at the speaker
  - they keep still
  - they think about the words being spoken.
- Younger children can be involved in non-verbal and verbal turn-taking games.
- Circle time games are useful to develop turn-taking; strategies such as the 'talk ticket' can also be helpful. This is when you can only talk if you are holding the talk ticket. This activity can be timed.
- Older children may need to be told the reason for the **rules of conversation**.
- The **rules** can be displayed on a wall; or put on a card; on the table/desk to remind a child that these rules are operating in a discussion situation. This is helpful for an older child – but all children must conform.
- Let the child know if he has not observed the **rules**. Rather than say 'no' , 'be quiet', 'wait' etc. give the child feedback in a neutral tone of voice, such as, 'David, listen until Lisa has finished', 'Not yet, I'm still talking', 'You haven't waited long enough yet', 'No, it's not your turn until Hayley has finished.'

Knowing when and how to join a conversation, and when to stop

The child having difficulties turn-taking will probably also have difficulty joining conversations appropriately. This is a difficult thing to learn if it does not come naturally. It may be helpful to have the '**rules of joining in**' made explicit.

- These are:
  - nod and agree with the speaker
  - stand by the person (not too close)

- wait for a pause (often the speaker's voice goes down just before the pauses)
- look at the person
- then ask a question or say something else about the same thing.

- The child needs to know he must indicate to the speaker an intention to join in, by looking, nodding, catching their eye.
- The child needs to learn not to interrupt, but also that in an emergency it is appropriate to do so. It can be useful for the children to decide what is 'polite' or 'helpful' interrupting and then all agree to stick to the same rules.
- The child needs to learn when to stop speaking. Some find this difficult and cannot read non-verbal cues such as embarrassed or bored expressions. They are best helped by being told a **'rule'**, such as stop after two or three sentences or points (or use an egg timer). The class could develop a signal to indicate 'too long', such as having a card shown or passed to the child who is talking for too long.
- The child needs to be aware that conversation is like a ball, to be passed to and fro, and that others must have a chance to respond.

Listening to others

Some children use their language primarily to express their own thoughts and are not especially interested in what others think or feel. For them, communication is not really a two-way activity, and genuine conversations are not particularly rewarding.

- The child needs to know that he will not be able to detect the correct time to join a conversation if he is not listening for the pauses.
- There are **'rules for good listening'**. These are:
  - look at the speaker
  - think about the same thing
  - don't 'switch off'
  - don't fidget.

It will be necessary to talk about the rules, and discuss why they are necessary.

- Help the child develop awareness of a listener's voice. Explain, or help them realise (through role play etc.) that the tone of voice can let others know about:
  - how the speaker feels (surprised, happy, sad)
  - how the speaker feels about who they are talking to (friendly, cross, superior)
  - how the speaker feels about what is being said (enthusiastic, bored, angry).

Developing conversation beyond one turn

Some children are very dependent on others, such as an adult, to move the conversation along. The adult needs to be aware if the child continues to only respond but not develop the conversation.

- Role play and drama may be useful. For instance, develop a scenario such as 'The Old Pirate'. The cabin boy wants to know where the dying pirate has buried the treasure. The child can be the cabin boy, the adult (or other child) the pirate who can only speak one or two words at a time. Or 'The Alien'. The child finds an ET-type character and tries to find out about his planet. Rehearse and repeat.

- In a group, ask each child to talk about their news. Each of the others has to ask him a question to which he has to respond. Take turns. Encourage further development of the conversation with comments like, 'Mark's been to Metroland too. Mark, tell Stephen what you liked best. Ask him what he liked.'
- Make absurd and silly remarks to provoke a response in the child so that he feels a need to know more. These could be things like:
    - I went to the moon on Saturday.
    - My purple dog has been very naughty.
    - Mrs Smith went to the shops and bought all the holes from inside Polo mints.
- Play verbal absurdity games.

Being aware of a listener's knowledge and needs

This is when the child does not know what you need to know in order to understand. It may be because the child assumes that if he knows it then you know it, and is unaware of what is and isn't shared knowledge. The child may not have given the necessary referents:

- to the place
- to the time
- to the people/things.

- In order to help him develop awareness you need to give feedback. Say (*not* critically) things such as, 'You haven't told me where this was.'
- Use role play to show how conversations break down, with the child as observer. Model unclear messages. Encourage the child to correct an unclear message so it can be understood.
- Use unclear messages such as, 'He was at my house last night.' (Who?) 'You remember that time I was hurt?' (When?) 'We went out to where I like to play.' (Where?) 'We played football by the stones.' (Which? Where?)
- Ask the child to reflect on what he has NOT said when misunderstandings happen.

Clarifying others' misunderstandings

Some children get angry when others don't understand them. Some say exactly the same words louder, other refuse to say it again. They may not be able to clarify misunderstandings without help. The child needs to know it is not his fault and that the listener plays a part as well and needs help. You need to show that you are interested and want to hear what he has to say.

Sometimes misunderstandings occur when the events are muddled up, such as when children do not have a sense of sequence. They may need to be helped to see that events have a beginning, middle and end.

- Practise putting pictures of sequences in order, such as dressing, growth sequences etc. (LDA cards (Learning Development Aids, Cambridge), cut-up cartoons).
- Encourage the child to use the words 'beginning', 'middle' and 'end'. Use words such as 'next', 'and then', alongside visual support.
- Use drama and role play to show sequences (the others guess) such as getting up, having breakfast, getting on a bus/into a car.
- Use storylines and mindmaps to plan spoken and written language activities.

The child may not have the necessary vocabulary either through lack of experience, difficulty acquiring concepts and vocabulary, or he may be experiencing a word-finding difficulty.

- The child needs encouragement (and time) to try to find the word he wants. However, it may be better to supply it and encourage repetition after modelling.
- The child may respond to prompting with initial sound(s), or by telling him what it rhymes with.
- The child may respond to connections by meaning, for instance, if he can't remember 'cauliflower' he may do if you say, 'You might eat this with cheese.'
- Where there is a breakdown, encourage the child to get the meaning over in another way, by saying what it is used for, or where it is found.
- Play naming and guessing games, such as, 'You find this in the kitchen (where). It is made of wood (what). It is for stirring (function).' Change roles.

Supplying further information when asked

Some children rely on others, particularly an adult, to manage a conversation. They say the minimum and then the adult asks for more information. Their expressive language skills may be poor and they may need help to expand their conversation.

- You could try asking the child to say two things he likes to eat, what he did at the party etc., encouraging him to link the ideas with 'and'.
- The child can ask another (or you, in a role play) for more information, for instance on what you did on Saturday. Encourage him to ask questions beginning with 'where', 'when', 'who', 'how', 'why'.
- Other ideas to expand expressive language can be found in the EG section (pp.88–89).

Knowing when he has misunderstood

Some children are unaware that they have misunderstood. You will need to find out why. The child may find the language too difficult, rate and/or volume inappropriate, level of comprehension expected too high, poor memory, or the child may be inattentive, distractible or distracted.

Some children are very aware they have misunderstood and can be lacking in confidence as a result.

- Try to encourage the child to tell you what he doesn't understand, or even why ('Amy was coughing', 'the bit about the coal being turned into carbon', 'that word for the gas', 'the last bit', 'what the question is').
- Encourage the child to:
    - be aware of the breakdown and reason
    - ask for clarification appropriately
    - be aware of what others are doing (not cheating)
    - not be afraid to ask for help.

Keeping to the topic

Some children are easily distracted and inattentive and need to be brought back to task frequently, and helped to stay on topic.

- It may help to bargain. 'Do this now and we'll talk about Thomas when the bell goes', 'Finish this and you can go on the computer at ten past three.'
- Reduce distractions in the classroom.

Giving relevant and appropriate responses

Children whose responses seem irrelevant may not have understood what has gone before, perhaps because of inattention, poor listening or because they have similar problems to those on the autistic spectrum and have an agenda of their own.

- Where the responses are inappropriate, teach the child who is in his close circle of family and friends, and who is not. Teach the child that a different style of behaviour is used for each group. What is appropriate for one group, such as teasing or swearing, is not suitable for another.
- Using the Conversation cue cards (pp.118–19) may help.

Understanding non-verbal cues

Facial expression and intonation do not help some children because they are unable to 'read' them.

- Teach the facial expressions that show basic emotions. Try using diagrams, pictures and photographs as well as modelling and role play. Staff should keep their own facial expressions and gestures clear and simple.
- Talk about the importance of eye contact. Practise looking for appropriate lengths of time in different situations. Try a system of verbal or visual prompting, e.g. 'look at me'.
- Teach the child about personal space around each one of us. Use visual cues and reminders and practise through modelling and role play, sitting and standing in an appropriate way in different situations. Allow the child to have his own space when necessary.
- Teach the child to associate body positions and posture with certain emotions by using photographs and role play.

Recognising the most important point

Some children 'cannot see the wood for the trees'. They get distracted by peripheral details. They may not see the point of what is happening – usually because they can't integrate the parts to make the whole picture. This is a problem of perception and integration. Many children with autistic spectrum disorders (ASD) have difficulties seeing the whole picture.

- You can help by 'cueing'. Ask questions designed to help him arrive at a conclusion, 'See the holly. When do we see holly berries?', 'See the table is set. Is it for one person or all the family?', 'See the crackers. When do we pull crackers?', 'When do we have a Christmas tree?', 'What are the people going to do next?', 'What day is it?'

- Developing better inferential skills may help – see RC section (pp.49–54).

Using an appropriate speech style

Some children, because of lack of social awareness, use speech styles inappropriately. Some children have 'adultified' speech, which can sound pompous and inappropriately authoritarian.

Some children have difficulty modulating the volume or varying the tone, while others don't know how to vary their response depending on the listener and context.

Making appropriate eye contact

Some children feel threatened by eye contact. Others don't know where to look for information – they may spend long periods looking at something inappropriate. Some children stare. This is a particular difficulty experienced by many children on the autistic spectrum.

- Point out and discuss why we look at a speaker:
  - it helps to keep your mind on the same subject
  - it tells you how the other person feels about what is being said (excited, bored, mocking)
  - it tells you how a person feels by looking at the face and expression, the eyes, the posture (sitting, standing, moving).
- Point out and discuss why you look at the person you are speaking to:
  - so you know if the other person understands you
  - so you know if the person is interested
  - so you can tell how the person feels about what you are saying
  - so you can change what or how you are saying it if the person doesn't seem to understand or be interested.
- Encourage the child to look for appropriate lengths of time; longer for some children, shorter periods for others.
- Encourage the child to look at the place where he will get most information. This may be where the other person is pointing, or where the other person's eyes are looking.
- Encourage the child to follow class conversations by looking at the different speakers when they speak.
- Play games like 'Wink Swap' and 'Pass the Smile' where the children have to look in each other's faces to play. Use the Conversation cue cards (pp.118–19).

CS4 Conversation cue cards

These are on pp.118–19.

- These can be glued to card and used as cue cards.
- They can be the focus for discussion in a group (or one-to-one).
- They are good as prompts for role play. One or two people can model how *not* to stick to the rules, as well as what to do.
- They have been found to be useful with older children especially. For instance, the card 'Working in a Group' has been used in small group situations, especially for group problem-solving activities in science. All children have had to comply with the rules.
- Some children have benefited from the visual prompts, especially those who have not learned the unwritten rules of conversation.

Conversation cue cards

LOOKING AT ANOTHER PERSON WHO IS SPEAKING

☐ helps you to keep your mind on the same subject
☐ tells you how the person feels about what is being said.

You can tell how a person feels by looking at:

☐ the face and expression
☐ the eyes
☐ the posture (how a person sits, stands and moves).

LOOKING AT ANOTHER PERSON WHILE YOU SPEAK

Tells you:

☐ if the person understands you
☐ if the person is interested in what you are saying
☐ how the person feels about what you are saying
☐ if you need to CHANGE anything so the person understands you better.

Things you might change:

☐ how fast you speak
☐ what tone you use
☐ how long you speak for – you will be able to see if the other person wants to ask you something or make a comment
☐ how much setting and context you need to give – if you haven't given enough the other person will be puzzled.

CONVERSATION means taking turns to speak

It means – listening to the other speakers
– taking turns to speak.

RULES OF CONVERSATION

1. Sit still, don't fidget.
2. Look at the speaker.
3. Think about the words.
4. Don't butt in.

IF YOU WANT TO JOIN IN

Nod and agree with the speaker.
Stand by the person.
Wait for a pause.
Look at the person.
Ask a question or talk about the same thing.

TURN-TAKING means giving everyone who wants the chance to speak.

It means you must not talk too long.
You must stop after you have made one or two points.
You must give the other person a chance to respond.

Conversation is like a ball – it has to be thrown backwards and forwards.

WORKING IN A GROUP

1. **NO-ONE IS MORE IMPORTANT** than anyone else.
2. **EVERYONE** should have something to do for part of the task.
3. **BRAINSTORM** for ideas of what to do, how to do it, what order to do it in.

A BRAINSTORM means **EVERYONE** gives ideas
BUT – all ideas are equally valid
    – no criticism is allowed.

If you CAN'T AGREE

☐   vote and accept the majority decision
☐   take turns to make decisions.

CRITICISM is GOOD when

☐   it is helpful
☐   it makes the other person feel better
☐   it is honest
☐   it doesn't hurt anyone's feelings.

CRITICISM is BAD when

☐   it is something that can't be changed such as how someone looks, how clever someone is, etc.
☐   it makes a person feel bad
☐   it is done in front of other people
☐   it is not clear so it is not helpful
☐   it doesn't tell you what to do to make things better
☐   it is not fair
☐   it is not honest.

CS5 Conversation skills: IEP targets

These should be **S**pecific, **M**easurable, **A**chievable, **R**elevant, **T**imed (i.e. **SMART**). Choose the most appropriate from the list below:

- **listen to other children talking** – *see CS1* (p.108–109), *CS3* (p.112) *and UL2*
- **initiate conversations with other children** – *see CS1* (p.108–9) *and CS3* (p.111)
- **join a conversation without interrupting** – *see CS3* (p.111–12)
- **take turns appropriately** – *see CS3* (p.111) *and CS4* (p.118–19)
- **develop a conversation beyond one turn** – *see CS3* (p.112–13)
- **develop awareness of a listener's knowledge** – *see CS3* (p.113–14)
- **clarify others' misunderstandings** – *see CS3* (p.113–14)
- **supply further information when asked** – *see CS3* (p.114)
- **keep to the topic under discussion** – *see CS3* (p.115)
- **develop awareness of non-verbal cues** – *see CS3* (p.115), *CS4* (p.118)
- **use an appropriate speech style** – *see CS3* (p.116)
- **develop appropriate eye contact/look at the speaker/maintain gaze** – *see CS3* (p.116) *and CS4* (p.118)
- **give relevant and appropriate responses in conversations** – *see CS3* (p.115)

(specify)
one-to one/with adult support/within a small group/whole class/independently.

Useful books and resources

We have found these resources informative and helpful. Many of these publishers have other very good materials apart from those mentioned, and are continually updating their lists.

Section 1: Receptive language difficulties

Language Gap. Senter. Freepost NT 255, Whitley Bay, NE26 1BR (success@senter.co.uk).

Semantic Links
Semantic Connections
Cambridge Language Activity Pack. STASS, 44 North Road, Ponteland, Northumberland NE20 9UR.

Living Language by Anne Locke. NFER-Nelson Ltd, Darville House, 2 Oxford Road East, Windsor SL4 1DF.

Words in Pictures
Sentence Builder
Black Sheep Press, 67 Middleton, Cowling, Keighley, W. Yorks BD22 0DQ.

Look, Listen and Think by Jean Edwards. Prim-Ed Publishing, PO Box 051, Nuneaton, Warwickshire CV11 6ZH (www.prim-ed.com).

Reading and Thinking
Finish the Story
Looking and Thinking
Sequencing Stories
Reading for Meaning
Learning Matters Limited, Dixon Street, Wolverhampton WV2 2BX (Learning.Materials@ btinternet.com).

Top Ten Thinking Tactics
Primary Thinking Skills Programme
Improving Thinking Skills through the Literacy Hour
by Mike Lake and Marjorie Needham. Questions Publishing, Leonard House, 321 Bradford Street, Birmingham B5 6ET (www.education-quest.co.uk).

CLIP Semantics Worksheets
CLIP Morphology Worksheets
CLIP Syntax Worksheet
The Psychological Corporation, Harcourt, 19500 Bulverde Road, San Antonio,Texas, USA (www.psychorp.com).

Section 2: Non-verbal difficulties

Improving Concentration Skills by Mike Lake and Majorie Needham.
Improving Memory Skills by Mike Lake and Angie Steele.
Questions Publishing, Leonard House, 321 Bradford Street, Birmingham B5 6ET
(www.education-quest.co.uk).

Listening Skills KS1 and KS2 by Sandi Rickerby and Sue Lambert. Questions Publishing,
Leonard House, 321 Bradford Street, Birmingham B5 6ET (www.education-quest.co.uk).

Functional Language in the Classroom and at Home by Maggie Johnson. The Commercial Office,
Manchester Metroplian University, Elizabeth Gaskell Site, Hathersage Road, Manchester
M13 0JA.

Section 3: Expressive language difficulties

Functional Language in the Classroom and at Home by Maggie Johnson. The Commercial Office,
Manchester Metroplitan University, Elizabeth Gaskell Site, Hatherstage Road, Manchester
M13 0JA.

The Selective Mutism Resource Manual by Maggie Johnson and Alison Wintgens. Speechmark
Publishing Ltd, Telford Road, Bicester, Oxon OX26 4LQ (www.speechmark.net).

Supporting Children with Speech and Language Impairment and Associated Difficulties by Jill
McMinn. Questions Publishing, Leonard House, 321 Bradford Street, Birmingham B5 6ET
(www.education-quest.co.uk).

Social Use of Language Programme by Wendy Rinaldi. NFER-Nelson Ltd, Darville House,
2 Oxford Road East, Windsor SL4 1DF.

Teaching Talking by Ann Locke. NFER-Nelson Ltd, Darville House, 2 Oxford Road East,
Windsor SL4 1DF.

PORIC: Language Concepts by Ginette Woods and Deborah Acers. Calender Nutsell Services,
Blake End, Essex CM7 8SH.

Socially Speaking by A. Schroeder. LDA, Duke Street, Wisbech, Cambs PE13 2AE (www.
1dallearning.com).

Practical Language Activities. ECL Publications, 798 West Solano Drive, Phoenix, Arizona,
USA 85013.

Talkabout: A Social Communications Package by A. Kelly. Speechmark Publishing, Telford Road,
Bicester, Oxon OX26 4LQ (www.speechmark.net).

A Place to Talk by Joan Tough. Ward Lock International.

CLIP Pragmatics Worksheets. The Psychological Corporation, Harcourt, 19500 Bulverde Road,
San Antonio, Texas, USA (www.psychorp.com).

Derbyshire Language Scheme. The Learning Support Division, Derbyshire County Council,
Ropley DE5 3BR.

The British Stammering Association. Information and support from 15 Old Ford Road, London
E2 9PJ.

AFASIC (for leaflets, booklets and support for parents). 2nd Floor, 50–52 Great Sutton Street,
London EC1V 0DJ.